Taxcafe Tax Guides

Pension Magic

How to Make the Taxman Pay for Your Retirement

By Nick Braun PhD

Important Legal Notices:

Published by:
Taxcafe UK Limited
2.4 West Bridge Mill
Kirkcaldy KY1 1TE

Email: team@taxcafe.co.uk

18th Edition, March 2026

ISBN 978-1-917392-09-9

Disclaimer
Before reading or relying on the content of this tax guide please read the disclaimer.

Disclaimer

1. This guide is intended as **general guidance** only and does NOT constitute accountancy, tax, financial, investment or other professional advice.

2. The author and Taxcafe UK Limited make no representations or warranties with respect to the accuracy or completeness of this publication and cannot accept any responsibility or liability for any loss or risk, personal or otherwise, which may arise, directly or indirectly, from reliance on information contained in this publication.

3. Please note that tax legislation, the law and practices by Government and regulatory authorities (e.g. HM Revenue & Customs) are constantly changing. We therefore recommend that for accountancy, tax, financial, investment or other professional advice, you consult a suitably qualified accountant, tax advisor, financial adviser, or other professional adviser.

4. Please also note that your personal circumstances may vary from the general examples given in this guide and your professional adviser will be able to give specific advice based on your personal circumstances.

5. This guide covers UK taxation only and any references to 'tax' or 'taxation', unless the contrary is expressly stated, refer to UK taxation only. Please note that references to the 'UK' do not include the Channel Islands or the Isle of Man. Foreign tax implications are beyond the scope of this guide.

6. All persons described in the examples in this guide are entirely fictional. Any similarities to actual persons, living or dead, or to fictional characters created by any other author, are entirely coincidental.

About the Author & Taxcafe

Dr Nick Braun founded Taxcafe in 1999, along with his partner Aileen Smith. As the driving force behind the company, their aim is to provide affordable plain-English tax information for private individuals, business owners and professional advisors.

Since then Taxcafe has become one of the best-known tax publishers in the UK and has won several prestigious business awards.

Nick has been a specialist tax writer since 1989, first in South Africa, where he edited the monthly *Tax Breaks* publication, and since 1999 in the UK, where he has authored several tax books including *Small Business Tax Saving Tactics* and *Salary versus Dividends*.

Nick also has a PhD in economics from the University of Glasgow, where he was awarded the prestigious William Glen scholarship and later became a Research Fellow.

Dedication

To Sandy, one of my two much loved sons.

Contents

Introduction

Let's get straight down to business. The main reason people put money into pensions is to SAVE TAX.

As a pension saver you enjoy three important tax reliefs:

- Income tax relief on your contributions – what I call buying investments at a 40% discount.

- Tax-free growth – all your income and capital gains are completely tax free.

- Tax-free cash – up to 25% of your pension savings can be taken as a tax-free lump sum. The rest is taxed as income.

If maximising tax relief is your priority, as it should be, there's a lot more to it than simply putting away a fixed amount each year.

You may wish to decide *how much* to invest, making bigger or smaller pension contributions in some years or none at all.

You may wish to consider *who* makes the contributions: you, your employer, or your spouse or partner.

You may also want to look at *when* is the best time to invest.

And, of course, you may want to know *why* you should even bother investing in a pension in the first place. For example, are pensions better than other investment vehicles like ISAs?

All of these important issues are addressed in this guide and I think you will be surprised by some of the results.

In Part 1 we examine how tax relief on pension contributions is calculated and how much you are allowed to invest.

A few years ago the annual allowance (the amount you can invest each year) was raised from £40,000 to £60,000. This was a welcome change but, as we shall discover, calculating the maximum pension contribution you *can* make is not as important as calculating the maximum pension contribution you *should* make to maximise your tax relief.

Over 200,000 people do not claim all the tax relief to which they are entitled, so we also examine how you can make a backdated tax relief claim and avoid other common mistakes that could cost you thousands of pounds.

Another welcome change was the scrapping the complicated and much hated lifetime allowance charge. Previously, if your pension pot exceeded the £1,073,100 lifetime allowance, you faced paying up to 55% tax on the excess. You can now save up as much money as you like in a pension, without fear of paying a tax penalty.

That's the good news. The bad news is a cap has been placed on the amount of tax-free cash you can take from pensions over your lifetime: £268,275 (25% of the old lifetime allowance).

However, as we shall discover, even if you've used up your entitlement to tax-free cash, additional pension contributions are still worth considering. You could end up with 33% more money than someone who puts their money in an ISA – and ISAs themselves are pretty good tax shelters!

New Allowances from 6th April 2024

The lifetime allowance has been replaced by two new allowances:

- The lump sum allowance – £268,275
- The lump sum and death benefit allowance – £1,073,100

Both limit the amount of any lump sum that can be paid out of your pension free from income tax. The lump sum allowance limits the amount of tax-free cash you can receive when you start accessing your pension savings. The lump sum and death benefit allowance potentially limits the amount of any tax-free lump sum your beneficiaries can receive, if you die before reaching age 75.

We take a closer look at these new allowances in Chapters 3 and 10.

There's also a third allowance called the overseas transfer allowance which applies to any pensions you transfer overseas. We do not discuss this allowance in this guide.

Pension Freedom

Prior to April 2015 the amount of money you could withdraw from your pension was tightly controlled. Most individuals' savings could only come out at a trickle, either through an annuity or something called "capped drawdown".

These restrictions have been lifted completely, giving pension savers more control over their money than they have ever had.

Once you reach the minimum retirement age (currently 55) you have complete freedom to withdraw as much or as little money as you like from your pension pot, whenever you like.

As a result, pension savers have the ability to control their tax bills, by making big pension withdrawals in some tax years and smaller withdrawals in others.

In Part 2 of this guide we explain all of the "Pension Freedom" changes and show you how to save thousands of pounds in both income tax and capital gains tax by timing your pension withdrawals carefully.

Inheritance Tax

At present most individuals' remaining pension savings are exempt from inheritance tax, which means they can be passed on to family members with no adverse tax penalties.

However, from 6th April 2027 pensions will be subject to inheritance tax. We take a closer look at the proposed changes in Chapter 10.

Because most readers probably expect to be alive on 6th April 2027, we will assume, when comparing pensions with alternative investments like ISAs in the pages that follow, that your pension savings are subject to inheritance tax.

However, it is important to note that full details of the proposed change have not been finalised. Draft legislation has been published but further changes could be made. Until then, anything we say about pensions and inheritance tax is simply our best guess as to how the tax will impact pension savers. However, a complete u-turn seems extremely unlikely: pensions will, almost certainly, become subject to inheritance tax from 6th April 2027.

Before the change was announced, pensions offered what some commentators called an unlimited inheritance tax shelter. This proposed change has therefore delivered a blow to some wealthier retirees who have been preserving their pension pots for their children and using other savings to fund their retirement.

However, it's important to point out that imposing inheritance tax on pensions will simply level the playing field – it will not make pensions less attractive than other assets or savings vehicles. In fact, as we shall see, in some cases a pension will still be better for passing wealth to family members.

And pensions are still fantastic *income tax* shelters for those who wish to use them for their intended purpose: to provide retirement income.

Pensions versus ISAs and Taxed Accounts

In Part 3 we show how pensions are usually much more powerful income tax shelters than ISAs. We track two investors over a number of years and reveal that a pension saver could end up with 41.67% more retirement income than an ISA investor.

Those under the age of 40 can currently open a Lifetime ISA and use it to save for either a first home or retirement. Part 3 tells you everything you need to know about this savings vehicle and why some taxpayers could end up with 17.6% more retirement income if they use a Lifetime ISA instead of a traditional pension.

Part 3 also contains a chapter for those who are already making full use of their £20,000 ISA allowance and have spare cash sitting in a taxed savings account or investment account. In one example we show how you could end up with 73% more money by sticking that cash in a pension.

Postponing & Accelerating Pension Contributions

In Part 4 we look at the pros and cons of postponing and accelerating pension contributions: making smaller than normal contributions or bigger than normal contributions.

This part of the guide has become more relevant than ever following the Government's recent decision to freeze income tax thresholds further until 5th April 2031.

Thanks to the freeze, more and more people are becoming higher-rate taxpayers and paying 40% income tax. We show how basic-rate taxpayers – those earning under £50,270 – may be able to increase their pension pots by 33% by postponing pension contributions for several years, until they become higher-rate taxpayers.

This part of the guide also contains a fascinating case study which reveals that, even if a higher-rate taxpayer postpones making pension contributions for several years (for example if they don't want to tie up savings in a pension), they will not necessarily end up one penny worse off than someone who makes pension contributions for many years.

One group that should consider making bigger than normal pension contributions are households where the highest earner's income is between £60,000 and £80,000 (or slightly over £80,000) and child benefit is being claimed.

As we shall see, by making pension contributions to reduce taxable income, people in this income bracket can typically enjoy tax relief of between 47% and 66%!

High Income Earners

Part 4 contains a special chapter for high income earners. High income earners include those with taxable income of £100,000 or more, as well as those getting close to £100,000.

When your income rises above £100,000 your personal allowance is gradually withdrawn. The end result is anyone in the £100,000 to £125,140 income bracket can enjoy 60% tax relief on their pension contributions.

And when your income rises above £125,140 you start paying tax at the 45% additional rate and can enjoy 45% tax relief on your pension contributions.

Additional-rate taxpayers can enjoy a combination of 45% tax relief and 60% tax relief if their pension contributions are big enough to reduce their 'adjusted net income' below £125,140. For example, someone who has taxable income of £140,000 and makes a £40,000 pension contribution can enjoy 54.4% tax relief.

There are a number of strategies high income earners can follow if they want to enjoy 60% tax relief or something close to 60%.

These include postponing pension contributions or making bigger than normal contributions in some tax years. These tax saving strategies are explored in detail.

This chapter also explains the special rules for the highest income earners who may be affected by the 'tapered annual allowance'.

Employees, Business Owners & Landlords

In Parts 5 to 7 we look at different types of pension saver: salaried employees, company owners, the self employed and landlords.

In Part 5 we explain 'auto-enrolment': the compulsory pensions that help many employees enjoy a pension contribution from their employer. Some individuals who can receive this free money from their employers may decide to opt out. So in this section we publish an interesting table which shows just how much bigger your pension pot will be if you take full advantage of pension contributions from your employer.

Chapter 24 in this part of the guide covers salary sacrifice pensions, which allow you to enjoy both income tax relief and *national insurance* relief on your pension contributions, including the 15% your employer pays. A salary sacrifice pension is arguably the most powerful tax-saving tool available to salaried employees.

However, as announced in the November 2025 Budget, the Government is placing a £2,000 cap on the amount of salary sacrifice pension contributions exempt from national insurance from 6th April 2029. Chapter 24 contains full details of this major change to employee pensions.

Part 6 covers company owners and directors and reveals why company pension contributions are now, more than ever, a highly tax-efficient way to extract money from your business. We also explain why getting your company to make the contributions is more tax efficient than making the contributions yourself.

There is also a chapter looking at the benefits and drawbacks of using your pension to make a loan to your company – you can do this if you have a small self-administered pension scheme (SSAS).

Most of this guide is relevant to the self employed (sole traders and business partners). Some additional practical pointers are provided in Part 7 to help this group maximise their tax relief.

I've also included a chapter for landlords. It shows how pension contributions may be tax efficient if your taxable property income pushes you into a higher tax bracket and covers some of the special issues faced by landlords making pension contributions.

Did you know that pension contributions can also provide *capital gains tax relief*, not just income tax relief? The chapter for landlords explains how pension contributions can reduce your capital gains tax rate from 24% to 18% when you sell property.

The final chapter in Part 7 looks at the pros and cons of putting commercial property into a pension.

Part 8 answers a key family pension planning question: "Who should make the pension contributions: me or my spouse/partner?" There is also a chapter looking at the pros and cons of opening a pension for your children or grandchildren.

Future Changes to Pension Tax Relief?

Most of this guide is based on the *current* tax rules affecting pensions. However, it's important to remember that pensions are long-term saving vehicles, which means some of the tax rules are likely to change while you are contributing to one. The recent inheritance tax announcement is a good example.

For many years newspapers have been reporting that the Government plans to reduce the income tax relief on pension contributions. Fortunately no such announcement has been made to date. However, we wouldn't be surprised to see a change at some point in the future.

For this reason some individuals, such as higher-rate taxpayers and additional-rate taxpayers, may wish to consider making the most of the current tax incentives while they are still available. Other individuals, for example basic-rate taxpayers, could end up better off if there are changes.

Readers should bear all this in mind when we talk about things like the benefits and drawbacks of postponing pension contributions. The tax rules could change!

I hope you find *Pension Magic* an enjoyable and interesting read.

Scope of this Guide

This guide does not cover every aspect of pension saving. The focus is *maximising income tax relief,* which is the main reason most people invest in the first place.

I do not cover issues like fees, how you should invest your money (in shares, equity funds, bonds, property etc), or how to choose a pension provider. I make no excuses for these omissions. As it is, I've struggled to keep the guide to a manageable size focusing on tax-saving strategies.

Nevertheless, it's important to point out that these other issues are extremely important. Annual account charges vary significantly from one pension provider to the next (from 0.35% of your pension pot to a fixed pound amount). If you invest in funds, the annual fees also vary considerably (for example, 0.95% for one popular managed fund compared with 0.08% for one well-known tracker fund).

There's no point maximising the tax relief on your pension contributions if you give away all these savings over time by paying high fees.

The focus of this guide is defined contribution pension schemes, also known as money purchase schemes. These include all individual pensions (for example, personal pensions and SIPPs) and most company pension schemes these days.

The basic idea is you (and your employer if you have one) put money in and the amount of income you get out at the end of the day depends on how well your investments have performed.

There is very little discussion of defined benefit (final salary) pension schemes. With this type of scheme your employer promises to pay you a pension based on your salary and years of service.

Final salary schemes are increasingly scarce in the private sector because employers are unwilling to pay someone a guaranteed level of income for the rest of their life. However, they are still the order of the day in the public sector, with the taxpayer picking up the tab.

Lifetime Allowance Protection

Before it was abolished, the lifetime allowance placed a cap on the amount of money you could save in pensions without incurring a tax charge.

The lifetime allowance was £1.8 million in 2011/12 but was steadily reduced to just £1 million in 2016/17. It was then increased with inflation to £1,073,100 before being scrapped.

When the lifetime allowance was being lowered, existing pension savers could apply for various forms of 'protection', which allowed them to benefit from the previously higher lifetime allowance and a bigger tax-free lump sum.

These protections are still relevant and allow some individuals to benefit from a lump sum allowance of more than £268,275 and a lump sum and death benefit allowance of more than £1,073,100 (we'll find out more about these allowances later on). However, we do not discuss any protection-related issues in this guide. The focus is on individuals whose pension pots are much smaller than the old lifetime allowance but want to grow their pension wealth in the years ahead.

We also do not discuss in any detail things like 'serious ill health lump sums' and some of the lump sum death benefits that affect the new allowances.

Scottish Taxpayers

Pensions are all about income tax and income tax in Scotland is different to the rest of the UK. Most of the information in this guide is relevant to Scottish taxpayers. However, unless stated to the contrary, all examples and calculations are based on the assumption that the taxpayer concerned is not a Scottish taxpayer.

Finally, please remember that this guide is not meant to be a substitute for proper professional advice. Before you act you should contact a suitably qualified accountant, tax advisor, financial advisor or pensions expert who understands your personal circumstances.

Part 1

Putting Money In: The Pension Contribution Rules

Chapter 1

Tax Relief on Contributions: How it's Calculated

When you make pension contributions the taxman will top up your savings by paying cash directly into your plan. Effectively for every £80 you invest, the taxman will put in an extra £20.

Why £20, you might be asking? Well your contributions are treated as having been paid out of income that has already been taxed at the 20% basic rate of income tax. The taxman is therefore refunding the income tax you've already paid.

The company that manages your pension plan – usually an insurance company or SIPP provider – will claim this money for you from the taxman and credit it to your account.

So whatever contribution you make personally, divide it by 0.80 and you'll get the total amount that is invested in your pension pot.

Example
Peter invests £4,000 in a self-invested personal pension (SIPP). After the taxman makes his top-up payment, the total amount of money Peter will have sitting in his pension pot is £5,000:

£4,000/0.80 = £5,000

Basic-rate tax relief isn't the end of the story. If Peter is a higher-rate taxpayer, paying tax at 40%, he'll be able to claim even more tax relief.

The Cherry on Top – Higher Rate Relief

A higher-rate taxpayer is someone who earns more than £50,270.

If you are a higher-rate taxpayer the taxman will let you claim your higher-rate tax relief when you submit your tax return.

Alternatively, if you are a company employee, higher-rate tax relief can be provided immediately by reducing the tax paid on your salary via your PAYE code.

(See Chapter 5 for more information on how to claim higher-rate tax relief.)

Example
As we already know, Peter's personal contribution is £4,000 and total pension fund investment, including the taxman's top-up, is:

£4,000/0.80 = £5,000

The £4,000 is what's known as the 'net contribution' and the £5,000 is what's known as the 'gross contribution'.

Multiplying the gross contribution by 20% we get:

£5,000 x 20% = £1,000

This is Peter's higher-rate tax relief.

Effectively he has a pension investment of £5,000 which has cost him just £3,000 (£4,000 personal contribution less his £1,000 tax refund). In other words, he is getting all of his investments at a 40% discount.

This is the critical number. Being able to make investments year after year at a 40% discount can have a huge effect on the amount of wealth you accumulate.

Tax Relief at More than 40%

Those with income falling into the following tax brackets can enjoy more than 40% tax relief on their pension contributions:

- £60,000-£80,000 47% or more
- £100,000-£125,140 60%
- £125,140 + 45%

The first tax bracket is where the child benefit charge applies. Pension contributions can help those affected reduce the charge or avoid it altogether (see Chapter 20).

The second tax bracket is where your personal allowance is withdrawn. 60% tax relief is available in this bracket and when your income rises above £125,140 you become an additional-rate taxpayer and 45% tax relief is available (see Chapter 21).

Basic-Rate Tax Relief – Time Delays

As mentioned earlier, your pension provider claims basic-rate tax relief from HMRC and adds it to your account. The delay could be anything from 6 to 11 weeks.

For example, looking at one well-known pension company, if you make a contribution between the 6th of March and 5th of April 2027 (inclusive) the tax relief will be paid into your account on the 21st of May 2027.

By timing your contributions carefully you can ensure that your basic-rate tax relief payments are received sooner rather than later. For example, a contribution made on the 1st of each month is better than a contribution made just after the 5th of each month.

Scottish Taxpayers 2026/27

Income tax in Scotland is being levied as follows in 2026/27:

£0 - £12,570	0%	Personal allowance (PA)
£12,570 - £16,537	19%	Starter rate
£16,537 - £29,526	20%	Basic rate
£29,526 - £43,662	21%	Intermediate rate
£43,662 - £75,000	42%	Higher rate
£75,000 - £100,000	45%	Advanced rate
£100,000 - £125,140	67.5%	PA withdrawal
Over £125,140	48%	Top rate

The higher-rate threshold, where 42% tax kicks in, remains £43,662. The top rate is 48% and a 45% 'advanced rate' affects those earning over £75,000.

The good news is Scottish taxpayers who find themselves in these tax brackets can enjoy 42%, 45% or 48% tax relief on their pension contributions. Those who find themselves in the £100,000-£125,140 income bracket can enjoy 67.5% tax relief on their contributions!

Scottish taxpayers who pay tax at just 19%, or pay no tax at all, continue to enjoy 20% tax relief on their pension contributions.

National Insurance Relief

Pensions provide income tax relief but generally no national insurance relief. However, it's important to point out that:

- Although there is generally no national insurance relief on pension contributions, there is also no national insurance payable on the income you eventually withdraw from your pension. For example, someone who earns a salary of £50,000 this year needs pension income of just £46,258 to end up with *exactly* the same after-tax income.

- If you are a higher-rate taxpayer your combined tax rate (income tax and national insurance) will be 42%. Pensions provide 40% tax relief which is pretty close to full tax relief.

- If you are a company owner you may not being paying any national insurance personally anyway. This will be the case if, like many, you pay yourself a salary no higher than the £12,570 primary threshold. As we shall see in Part 6, it is often more tax efficient for company owners to get their companies to make pension contributions, instead of making them personally. There is no national insurance payable on company pension contributions in these circumstances.

- Although there is generally no national insurance relief on pension contributions, there is one important exception: salary sacrifice pensions. We cover these in Chapter 24.

Summary

- When you make pension contributions you may be able to enjoy two types of income tax relief: Basic-rate tax relief which comes in the shape of top-ups to your pension plan and higher-rate relief which is normally claimed when you submit your tax return.
- Your total pension fund investment is found by dividing your personal contribution by 0.80. The taxman's top-up is paid directly to your pension provider who will credit your pension pot.
- Higher-rate relief is calculated by multiplying your gross pension contribution by 20%.
- Together these two tax reliefs mean all your pension investments come in at a 40% discount.
- Additional-rate taxpayers enjoy 45% tax relief and those in the £100,000-£125,140 or £60,000-£80,000 tax brackets may be able to enjoy even higher rates of tax relief.
- There is generally no national insurance relief on pension contributions.

Chapter 2

How Much Can You Invest?

In this chapter we will examine the rules that determine how much you can invest in a pension each year.

Successive governments have continually tampered with the pension system, for better or worse. If you are making pension contributions over several decades you should not rely on the same set of rules applying in 5, 10 or 20 years' time. The good news, for now at least, is that most individuals can make big enough pension contributions and enjoy full income tax relief.

Age

This is a good one to kick off with. Anyone who is *under 75* can make pension contributions which enjoy income tax relief. Pension contributions are allowed after reaching 75 but do not qualify for tax relief and many pension companies will not accept them.

In the March 2014 Budget the Government announced that it would explore whether this age limit should be changed or abolished. Following consultation, it was decided not to make any changes, so the age limit remains at 75.

There is effectively no lower age limit. You may not be able to set up your own pension plan if you're under 18 years of age but some pension providers have special products so that parents and grandparents can make pension contributions for their children and grandchildren (see Chapter 34 for more information).

Multiple Pension Schemes

A number of years ago many members of workplace schemes could not contribute to a second pension, such as a self-invested personal pension (SIPP). This is no longer the case. Most people can now contribute to more than one pension and have more control over how their retirement savings are invested.

The Basic Pension Contribution Rule

To obtain tax relief on your pension contributions they have to stay within certain limits:

- **Earnings**. Contributions made by you *personally* must not exceed your annual earnings.

- **The £60,000 Annual Allowance.** Total pension contributions by you and anyone else (normally your employer) must not exceed £60,000 per year. The annual allowance is reduced once you start withdrawing taxable income from your pension (see below). It may also be reduced if your "adjusted income" exceeds £260,000 (see Chapter 21 for more details).

The annual allowance was increased from £40,000 to £60,000 as part of a package of pension measures announced in the March 2023 Budget. The new allowance has applied since 6th April 2023.

Ignoring any employer contributions, an individual with earnings of £35,000 can contribute £35,000 to a pension with tax relief. An individual with earnings of £75,000 can contribute £60,000 (contributions capped by the annual allowance).

Employer contributions also have to be thrown into the mix when calculating the maximum pension contribution. Let's say the individual with earnings of £75,000 is an employee and his employer contributes £10,000 to his pension. The maximum contribution he can make personally is £50,000:

£60,000 annual allowance – £10,000 from employer = £50,000

How Relevant Is this to Me?

Almost everyone making pension contributions needs to understand what is meant by the term 'earnings'. Earnings are not the same as income. The annual allowance does not affect most people because most of us do not have anything close to £60,000 paid into our pension plans each year. However, as we shall see in Part 4, there may be times when you want to make big catch-up contributions. In these circumstances it is important to know a bit more about how the annual allowance operates.

Gross vs Cash Contributions

The above pension contribution limits are for *gross* pension contributions. However, the money you actually pay into your pension is normally NOT a gross pension contribution (unless you belong to certain types of occupational pension scheme). To calculate your gross contributions you have to add on basic-rate tax relief (the taxman's top up). You do this by dividing your actual cash contribution by 0.80.

How does this affect the pension contribution limits? If you have earnings of £35,000 you cannot pay £35,000 into your pension plan and receive tax relief. You can only pay in £28,000 (£35,000 x 0.8). The taxman will add a further £7,000 in tax relief, bringing your total gross pension contribution to £35,000.

Similarly, the £60,000 annual allowance is a cap on total gross pension contributions. So the maximum cash pension contribution an individual can make in the absence of any employer contributions is £48,000 (£60,000 x 0.8), with the taxman adding a further £12,000 in tax relief.

Employer Contributions

Contributions by employers are always gross contributions. When your employer puts money into your pension plan there is no additional top up from the taxman. Instead the company obtains tax relief by claiming employee pension contributions as a tax deductible business expense.

So if your employer contributes £10,000 to your pension this will be a gross contribution and the maximum gross contribution you can make personally is £50,000:

£60,000 – £10,000 = £50,000

The maximum amount you can actually pay into your pension plan would then be £40,000:

£50,000 x 0.8 = £40,000

You can only receive tax relief on this contribution if you have earnings of at least £50,000.

Occupational Pension Schemes

For many employees who belong to occupational schemes, the actual pension contribution is the same as the gross pension contribution.

Under the 'net pay arrangement' the employer deducts the employee's pension contributions from the employee's gross pay *before* tax is deducted. This means full tax relief is obtained immediately by paying the contribution out of pre-tax income. There is no top up by the taxman and no need to claim higher-rate tax relief via a tax return.

(Similarly, Scottish employees who pay tax at 21% or more do not have to claim back their additional tax relief from HMRC if they belong to a net pay arrangement – see previous chapter.)

Not all contributions by employees are made gross. If the employer has a pension scheme that uses 'relief at source' (usually group personal pensions), the employee's contributions are paid after the employee's salary has been taxed. Basic-rate relief is then claimed by the pension scheme and added to the member's pension pot to obtain their total gross pension contribution.

Earnings

To obtain tax relief on your pension contributions you have to have earnings – 'relevant UK earnings' to be precise.

Employees

If you are an employee, your relevant UK earnings will include:

- Salary or wages
- Bonus, overtime, and commissions, and
- Taxable benefits in kind

There are a few other bits and bobs that can count as relevant UK earnings for pension contribution purposes, including redundancy payments that exceed the £30,000 tax-free threshold and statutory sick pay and statutory maternity pay.

Company Directors

Most small company owners are also directors. For pension contribution purposes company directors are treated just like regular employees. Their relevant UK earnings include their salary, bonus, overtime, commissions and taxable benefits in kind.

As shareholders of their companies they can also pay themselves dividends. To save tax and national insurance, many company owners take a small tax-free salary and the rest of their income as dividends.

This year (2026/27) it is tax efficient for many company owners to pay themselves a salary of £12,570 and take the rest of their income as dividends (see Chapter 26).

The problem, however, is dividends are NOT earnings. As such, a company director with a salary of £12,570 and dividends of £50,000 can only contribute £12,570 to a pension with tax relief.

The actual cash contribution would be £10,056 (£12,570 x 0.8) with the taxman adding £2,514 in tax relief for a gross contribution of £12,570.

Fortunately for company owners, they can get their companies to make pension contributions (employer contributions) and these are not restricted to their earnings (although they are restricted by the £60,000 annual allowance). We'll take a closer look at pension planning for company owners in Part 6.

The Self-Employed

Most people would regard any business owner as 'self-employed'. However, when HMRC talks about 'self-employed' individuals they are referring specifically to owners of unincorporated businesses, in other words businesses that are not companies.

The most common are sole traders (one-person businesses) and partnerships.

If you are a sole trader your relevant UK earnings are generally the pre-tax profits of the business. If you are a partner, your relevant UK earnings will be your share of the partnership's pre-tax profit.

The problem is that many self-employed individuals don't know what their pre-tax profits are!

Most have an accounting period that is the same as the tax year, running to 5th April each year or 31st March. This can create a practical problem when it comes to maximising tax relief on pension contributions.

Although most salary earners (including company directors) have earnings that are fairly predictable (their salaries), the exact profits on which self-employed business owners can base their pension contributions may not be known until the accounts are drawn up *after* the tax year has ended.

In other words, as a self-employed business owner you may only know what your relevant UK earnings are when it is too late to make pension contributions. You cannot make back-dated pension contributions after the tax year has ended.

Income but Not Earnings

Earnings do not include:

- Rental income
- Interest
- Dividends
- Capital gains

For example, if you have earnings of £30,000 and rental income of £20,000 from buy-to-let properties, the maximum gross pension contribution you can make with tax relief is £30,000.

Individuals with No Earnings

Some people don't have any earnings, including non-working spouses and minor children.

Many professional landlords, who derive all of their income from rental properties, will also not have any earnings.

The good news is that everyone under the age of 75 can make a pension contribution of £3,600 per year, regardless of earnings.
The actual cash contribution would be £2,880, with the taxman adding £720 to bring the total gross contribution to £3,600.

We'll take a closer look at the pros and cons of making pension contributions when you have no earnings in Part 8.

The Annual Allowance

The annual allowance is the overall cap on the amount of pension contributions you can make with tax relief. It used to be £40,000 and was fixed at this level for almost a decade. However, it was increased to £60,000 with effect from 6th April 2023.

Your annual allowance is reduced once you start withdrawing taxable income from your pension (see below).

Your annual allowance is also reduced if your "adjusted income" exceeds £260,000 (see Chapter 21 for more details).

The annual allowance includes pension contributions made by both you and anyone else (normally your employer).

If your contributions exceed the annual allowance, you can carry forward unused allowance from the three previous tax years.

If the annual allowance is exceeded, and the excess is not covered by carry forward, the excess is taxed at your marginal income tax rate (typically 40% or 45%).

This annual allowance charge can be paid when you submit your tax return or deducted from your pension savings if it's over £2,000.

In practice, the £60,000 annual allowance is generous enough for most people and very few are affected by it. Those who have to be most careful are those making big one-off pension contributions.

Another group that has to be careful are members of final salary pension schemes (also known as defined benefit pension schemes).

The value of their pension benefits could increase by more than £60,000 in the year they receive a substantial pay increase. Professional advice should be obtained in these circumstances.

Pension Input Periods

A number of years ago, when calculating whether the annual allowance was exceeded, you didn't count pension contributions made during a *tax year* (5th April to 6th April). Instead you used the pension scheme's annual *pension input period*.

As a result, quite big pension contributions made during two different tax years could have fallen into just one pension input period and exceeded the annual allowance.

However, with effect from 6th April 2016 all pension input periods are now aligned with the tax year.

The Carry Forward Rule

If you want to make a big pension contribution that exceeds the annual allowance you can tap any unused allowance from the three previous tax years.

This means that someone who hasn't made any pension contributions so far during the current tax year can potentially make a pension contribution of up to £240,000 in 2026/27 and enjoy full tax relief:

- £60,000 for 2026/27
- £60,000 for 2025/26
- £60,000 for 2024/25
- £60,000 for 2023/24

Example
Paula is a sole trader and expects to make bumper taxable profits of £180,000 during the 2026/27 tax year.

She transfers £90,000 into her pension plan, resulting in a gross pension contribution of £112,500 (£90,000/0.8).

Her gross pension contributions in the three previous tax years were:

	Pension Contribution	*Unused Annual Allowance*
2025/26	*£30,000*	*£30,000*
2024/25	*£30,000*	*£30,000*
2023/24	*£20,000*	*£40,000*

In total Paula has £100,000 of unused annual allowance from the three previous tax year.

Together with the £60,000 annual allowance for the current tax year, Paula can make a total gross pension contribution of up to £160,000.

Her £112,500 gross pension contribution is therefore within the limits and does not exceed her earnings and therefore enjoys full tax relief.

You use the annual allowance for the current tax year first. You then use your unused annual allowance from the *earliest* tax year first (2023/24).

This leaves any unused allowance from the most recent tax years free to carry forward.

In Paula's case, after using her £60,000 allowance for the current 2026/27 tax year she has £52,500 of pension contributions remaining (£112,500 minus £60,000).

After using her remaining annual allowance from 2023/24 she will have £12,500 of pension contributions remaining (£52,500 minus £40,000).

After setting this off against her £30,000 remaining annual allowance from 2024/25 she will have £17,500 of annual allowance left from 2024/25 to carry forward to next year (£30,000 minus £12,500).

She will also have £30,000 of unused annual allowance from 2025/26 to carry forward to next year.

Earnings Can't Be Carried Forward

To enjoy tax relief, the pension contributions you make personally cannot exceed your earnings for the current tax year.

Although you can carry forward unused annual allowance, you cannot carry forward earnings from previous years or make backdated pension contributions.

Membership of a Pension Scheme Required

Unused annual allowance can only be carried forward if you were a member of a registered pension scheme for the period in question. For example, if you start contributing to a pension now but did not belong to any pension scheme in the three previous tax years, you cannot carry forward any unused annual allowance from those years.

On a practical level, this means that someone who does not currently have a pension plan in place, but may wish to make big contributions in a few years' time, should consider setting one up as soon as possible.

Getting your Contribution Right

The pension contribution rules are quite complex... but only if you have quite big contributions and are in danger of exceeding the annual allowance.

Most people will not have £60,000 per year added to their pension pots and are unaffected by the annual allowance rules (individuals who want to make big catch-up contributions are an important exception – see Chapter 19).

The earnings restriction is also irrelevant for the vast majority of people. Most would never contemplate contributing anything close to 100% of their earnings to a pension. (Company directors are one exception because they often pay themselves a small tax-free salary and therefore have very low 'earnings'.)

I don't want to sound flippant but it's important not to become bogged down by rules that may never affect you. Calculating the maximum pension contribution you *can* make is not the important issue for most people. What is far more important is calculating the maximum pension contribution you *should* make.

For those who are higher-rate taxpayers it may be more important to calculate the maximum pension contribution that will obtain full higher-rate tax relief. This is the subject of Chapter 4.

For those earning over £100,000 (and have their income tax personal allowance withdrawn) a more important calculation may be the pension contribution that will enjoy tax relief of up to 60% (see Chapter 21).

Take Paula in the above example. She has taxable profits of £180,000 and makes a gross pension contribution of £112,500. As we shall see in Chapter 21, the first £54,860 of her contribution reduces her 'adjusted net income' from £180,000 to £125,140 and enjoys 45% tax relief. The next £25,140 reduces her adjusted net income from £125,140 to £100,000 and enjoys 60% tax relief.

However, the final £32,500 of her contribution may only enjoy 40% tax relief. Thus she may be better off reducing her contribution this year by £32,500 if she thinks she will be able to enjoy more tax relief in a future tax year.

Contributions after Withdrawals Have Started

When you start withdrawing *income* from your pension, over and above your tax-free lump sum, your ability to make further pension contributions could be restricted.

You may no longer be entitled to a £60,000 annual allowance. Instead your contributions could be limited to just £10,000 per year. This is known as the 'money purchase annual allowance'.

If you have to withdraw income from your pension (for example during a period of financial hardship), rebuilding your retirement savings could be a lot more challenging if you are limited to a contribution of just £10,000 per year.

There are other anti-avoidance rules designed to prevent money being taken out of a pension in order to make new pension contributions, thereby benefiting from two rounds of tax relief.

If you use your tax-free lump sum to significantly increase your pension contributions, the contributions may fall foul of HMRC's recycling rules and a tax charge of up to 70% could be imposed.

We'll take a closer look at both these issues in Part 2 which deals with taking money out of pensions.

Chapter 3

The New Lump Sum Allowance

The lifetime allowance has been scrapped.

Previously, if your pension pot exceeded the £1,073,100 lifetime allowance, you faced paying a tax charge of up to 55% on the excess.

This lifetime allowance charge was scrapped on 6th April 2023 and the lifetime allowance itself was removed from the pension legislation on 6th April 2024.

As a result you can now save up as much money as you like in a pension to fund your retirement, without fear of paying a tax penalty.

However, it's important to point out that the amount of tax-free cash you can take HAS been capped – at £268,275.

The £268,275 Lump Sum Allowance

One of the main tax benefits of pensions is you can take 25% of your savings as a tax-free lump sum. Anything else you withdraw is subject to income tax.

When the scrapping of the lifetime allowance was announced, we were also told that the maximum amount of tax-free cash you can take will remain at £268,275, which is 25% of the old lifetime allowance:

£1,073,100 x 25% = £268,275

The previous Conservative Government also stated that this Lump Sum Allowance will remain frozen at £268,275. It will not automatically increase with inflation, so its real value is likely to fall over time.

It seems very unlikely the current Labour government will increase it.

Placing a cap on tax-free lump sums means that, even though the 55% lifetime allowance charge has been scrapped, there is still an *indirect* penalty for saving too much in pensions.

Having a pension pot bigger than £1,073,100 is NOT the same as having a pension pot smaller than £1,073,100.

However, as we shall see in the examples that follow, even without the benefit of tax-free cash, making additional pension contributions may still be worth considering.

Example – Higher-rate Taxpayer

Justus invests an extra £800 in his pension and the taxman adds £200 of basic-rate tax relief, giving him a gross pension contribution of £1,000. He also receives higher-rate tax relief of £200 which means the £1,000 investment costs him just £600. (See Chapter 1 for more information about how pension tax relief is calculated.)

Let's also assume that Justus's friend Kevin invests £600 in an ISA – the exact same amount Justus ends up investing personally (taking into account his higher-rate tax relief).

Now let's look at what happens when Justus and Kevin withdraw this money. To keep the example simple we can ignore investment growth because both pensions and ISAs enjoy tax-free growth. In other words, we will assume that Justus will have £1,000 to withdraw and Kevin will have £600 to withdraw.

Let's assume that Justus's previous pension savings will use up his £268,275 Lump Sum Allowance. In other words, he will pay income tax on the entire £1,000 withdrawal.

The key question then is: how much income tax will Justus pay? The figures below show how much he will be left with if he pays income tax at the 20% basic rate, the 40% higher rate or the 45% additional rate:

Income tax	***After tax***	***Versus ISA***
20%	*£800*	*+33%*
40%	*£600*	*Identical*
45%	*£550*	*-8%*

If Justus already has pension income and other income that take him over the higher-rate threshold (currently £50,270), he will pay 40% tax when he withdraws this additional contribution. He will be left with £600 – exactly the same as Kevin the ISA investor.

If he only pays 20% tax, because his total taxable income does not exceed the higher-rate threshold, he will end up with 33% more money than Kevin. And if he pays 45% tax he will end up 8% worse off than Kevin.

What this example shows is that, even if without the benefit of tax-free cash, additional pension contributions may be worth making, as long as you expect to pay income tax at the same rate or at a lower rate when you withdraw the money.

Even if Justus expects to pay 40% tax when he withdraws the additional contribution he will still end up in exactly the same after-tax position as an ISA investor... and ISAs are pretty decent tax shelters!

Like Kevin the ISA investor, he will benefit from tax-free growth on his additional pension contribution. In other words, he will not have to pay any income tax on the interest or dividend income his pension contribution generates and he will not have to pay capital gains tax if the investments rise in value.

The tax-free growth offered by pensions and ISAs has become more valuable than ever following recent cuts to various tax-free allowances.

The annual capital gains tax exemption has been reduced to £3,000 (it used to be £12,300) and the annual dividend allowance has been cut to just £500 (it was £5,000 when first introduced but was steadily reduced).

Finally, note that making additional pension contributions in these circumstances may only be worth considering if you are already making full use of your £20,000 ISA allowance. It's probably not a good idea to save exclusively in a pension because ISAs have a number of advantages, including immediate access to your savings.

Inheritance Tax

At present pension savings are typically free from inheritance tax in most cases. However, this is set to change from 6th April 2027: pensions are expected to become subject to inheritance tax from this date.

What this means is that making additional pension contributions, simply for inheritance tax planning purposes, is now a less attractive proposition.

Most of this guide is about using pension contributions to provide you with *retirement income*. However, we'll take a closer look at pensions and inheritance tax in Chapter 10.

Additional-rate Taxpayers

In the above example Justus was a higher-rate taxpayer when he made his additional pension contribution.

However, it is arguably additional-rate taxpayers (those who earn more than £125,140 and pay 45% tax) who are more likely to build up a pension pot worth more than £1,073,100 and thus have their entitlement to tax-free cash restricted.

Example – Additional-rate Taxpayer

Justus invests an extra £873 in his pension and the taxman adds £218 of basic-rate tax relief, giving him a gross pension contribution of £1,091. He also receives additional-rate tax relief of £273 which means the £1,091 investment costs him just £600.

(In Chapter 1 we saw that higher-rate tax relief is calculated by multiplying the gross pension contribution by 20%. Additional-rate relief is calculated by multiplying the gross contribution by 25%.)

Again we assume Justus's friend Kevin invests £600 in an ISA.

And again we assume that Justus's existing pension savings will use up his £268,275 Lump Sum Allowance, so he will pay income tax on the entire £1,091 when it is withdrawn.

The figures below show how much Justus will be left with depending on whether he pays income tax at 20%, 40% or 45%:

Income tax	***After tax***	***Versus ISA***
20%	*£873*	*+46%*
40%	*£655*	*+9%*
45%	*£600*	*Identical*

If Justus pays less than 45% tax when he withdraws the money from his pension he'll be left with more money than Kevin the ISA investor. Even if Justus pays 45% tax he'll be left with exactly the same amount of money as from an ISA investment.

Pensions versus ISAs

In the above examples we saw that, even if you expect your existing pension savings to grow to £1,073,100 and use up your £268,275 Lump Sum Allowance, additional pension contributions may still be worth considering. There's a good chance you'll end up in exactly the same after-tax position as putting your money in an ISA instead. You may end up better off.

Certainly additional pension contributions are worth considering if you are already making full use of your £20,000 annual ISA allowance. There's a good chance you will pay income tax and capital gains tax on your income and gains if your investments are held outside both an ISA and pension.

However, if you are NOT already making full use of your ISA allowance the decision is more complicated. Personally, I'm not convinced making additional pension contributions is worth considering unless you are already making full use of your ISA allowance.

ISAs give you instant access to your savings, regardless of your age, and protect you from any future increase in income tax rates. Having a combination of ISA and pension savings is probably a fairly prudent way to spread your risk.

The Lump Sum Allowance – Further Details

The £268,275 Lump Sum Allowance is a lifetime limit and applies to the totality of your pension savings – you cannot withdraw £268,275 tax free from each pension scheme you belong to.

Whenever tax-free cash is taken, this will reduce your available Lump Sum Allowance. You don't have to take all your tax-free cash in one go. You can withdraw it in dribs and drabs.

The types of withdrawal that will use up your allowance include:

- Pension commencement lump sums (PCLS). This is the formal name for the tax-free lump sums (or tax-free cash) most people receive when they start accessing their pension savings. For example, if you crystallise £100,000 of your pension savings and take 25% tax-free cash of £25,000, with the remaining £75,000 placed into a drawdown account, your Lump Sum Allowance will be reduced by £25,000, leaving you with £243,275.

- The tax-free element of an Uncrystallised Funds Pension Lump Sum (UFPLS). The tax-free element is typically 25% of the total amount withdrawn, with the rest taxed as income. For example, if you take a UFPLS of £20,000 your Lump Sum Allowance will be reduced by £5,000, leaving you with £263,275.

These lump sum withdrawals are referred to in the industry as "relevant benefit crystallisation events". We will take a closer look at drawdown and UFPLS in Chapter 8.

Pension Benefits Taken Before 6th April 2024

If you accessed your pension before 6th April 2024 (under the old lifetime allowance regime), your starting Lump Sum Allowance (LSA) can be worked out with the following standard calculation:

- Take the total lifetime allowance % used (40%, 80% etc)
- Multiply this % by £1,073,100
- Multiply this amount by 25% to give the LSA already used
- Deduct this from your starting LSA (typically £268,275)

If you used all of your lifetime allowance before 6th April 2024 you will generally have no Lump Sum Allowance remaining.

Example – Lifetime allowance £1,073,100

Ruta crystallised £429,240 of her pension savings in 2022/23 when the lifetime allowance was £1,073,100, using 40% of the lifetime allowance. She received a tax-free lump sum of £107,310. Her Lump Sum Allowance is reduced by:

£1,073,100 x 40% x 25% = £107,310

Remaining Lump Sum Allowance £160,965: £268,275 less £107,310.

Example – Lifetime allowance £1,250,000

Emilia crystallised £600,000 of her pension savings in 2015/16 when the lifetime allowance was £1,250,000, using 48% of the lifetime allowance at the time. She received a tax-free lump sum of £150,000. She has no lifetime allowance protection. Her Lump Sum Allowance is reduced by:

£1,073,100 x 48% x 25% = £128,772

Remaining Lump Sum Allowance £139,503: £268,275 less £128,772.

Example – Lifetime allowance £1 million

John crystallised £600,000 of his pension savings in 2017/18 when the lifetime allowance was £1 million, using 60% of the lifetime allowance at the time. He received a tax-free lump sum of £150,000. He has no lifetime allowance protection. His Lump Sum Allowance is reduced by:

£1,073,100 x 60% x 25% = £160,965

Remaining Lump Sum Allowance £107,310: £268,275 less £160,965.

Note John's Lump Sum Allowance is reduced by more than the tax-free cash he actually withdrew from his pension.

People like John who have taken less tax-free cash from their pensions than this default calculation assumes can apply to their pension scheme for a 'transitional tax-free amount certificate', which may allow them to enjoy a larger starting Lump Sum Allowance.

If John makes a successful application his starting Lump Sum Allowance will be £118,275 instead of £107,310.

The certificate must be obtained before the first relevant benefit crystallisation event occurs after 5th April 2024.

To make a successful application it is necessary to provide complete documentary evidence of all the tax-free lump sums that have been taken, along with the lifetime allowance usage.

Individuals who may benefit from one of these certificates include those who took tax-free cash between 6th April 2016 and 5th April 2020 when the lifetime allowance was less than £1,073,100.

Others who may benefit include individuals who have used up some or all of their lifetime allowance but did not take the full amount of tax-free cash they were entitled to (for example, some members of defined benefit pension schemes).

Some people could be worse off with a transitional tax-free amount certificate. If you've always taken 25% as tax-free cash and didn't crystallise any of your pension savings when the lifetime allowance was less than £1,073,100, obtaining a certificate will probably not give you a higher Lump Sum Allowance.

If you took a tax-free lump sum when the lifetime allowance was greater than £1,073,100, like Emilia in the above example, applying for a certificate could put you in a worse position. The default calculation will probably produce a better outcome.

Lump Sum and Death Benefit Allowance

The Lump Sum and Death Benefit Allowance is the second major allowance that has replaced the lifetime allowance.

It typically places a limit on the amount of any lump sum that can be paid to your family free from income tax, if you die before age 75. It also limits the amount of any tax-free lump sum that can be paid out to someone under age 75 and in 'serious ill health'.

For most people the Lump Sum and Death Benefit Allowance is £1,073,100, less any tax-free cash already taken.

We'll take a closer look at this allowance in Chapter 10.

Lifetime Allowance Protection

Every time the lifetime allowance was reduced in the past it was possible to apply to protect your entitlement to the previous, higher lifetime allowance and higher tax-free lump sum.

Your lump sum allowance may be higher if you have lifetime allowance protection. These protections are beyond the scope of this guide and I recommend taking professional advice where relevant.

Chapter 4

How to Maximise Your Higher-Rate Tax Relief

Everyone who makes pension contributions enjoys basic-rate tax relief (the taxman's 20% top up). If you are a higher-rate taxpayer you can also claim an additional 20% tax relief.

However, some higher-rate taxpayers don't enjoy full tax relief on their pension contributions because they don't understand how higher-rate relief is calculated. It's a bit like paying for a business class ticket and accidentally sitting in economy.

What is a Higher-Rate Taxpayer?

A higher-rate taxpayer is someone with taxable income of more than £50,270 (see below for Scottish taxpayers). The threshold normally increases with inflation but has been frozen for an astonishing 10 years until the end of the 2030/31 tax year on 5th April 2031.

This means many basic-rate taxpayers are becoming higher-taxpayers, even if their income is simply increasing because of inflation. Similarly, individuals who are already higher-rate taxpayers are seeing a larger chunk of their income taxed at 40%, even though they are no better off in real terms.

On a more positive note, many pension savers can protect themselves from this tax increase by making pension contributions which enjoy higher-rate tax relief.

How Is Higher-Rate Relief Calculated?

When you make pension contributions the taxman gives you a bigger basic-rate band which means more of your income is taxed at 20% instead of 40%. Your basic-rate band is increased by the same amount as your *gross* pension contributions.

Example
Sandy is a sole trader with pre-tax profits of £57,000. He has £6,730 of income taxed at 40% (£57,000 - £50,270).

He puts £5,000 into a pension. The taxman adds £1,250 of basic-rate relief for a gross contribution of £6,250 (£5,000/0.8).

To calculate his higher-rate relief his basic-rate band is increased by £6,250, allowing £6,250 of income to be taxed at 20% instead of 40%. This saves Sandy £1,250 in tax (£6,250 x 20%).

This is the best possible outcome. Sandy has received basic-rate and higher-rate tax relief on his entire pension contribution. In total he enjoys 40% tax relief:

(£1,250 + £1,250) / £6,250 = 40%

The Maximum Higher Rate Relief

The maximum higher-rate tax relief you can claim is:

Your Gross Pension Contribution x 20%

However, you will only enjoy the maximum higher-rate tax relief if you have at least this much income taxed at 40%.

If your income is £50,270 plus one pound, you will only get higher-rate tax relief on one pound of pension contributions.

Sandy, whose income is £57,000, can enjoy higher-rate tax relief on a gross pension contribution of up to £6,730 (£57,000 – £50,270). His actual gross pension contribution is £6,250 so he has stayed within the limits. If he contributes more than £6,730, the additional contribution will only receive basic-rate relief.

Tax Planning

Big pension contributions can be a bad idea if you don't have enough income taxed at 40%.

To enjoy the maximum tax relief you may wish to consider spreading your pension contributions over a number of tax years.

If maximising tax relief is your priority, you should make sure your gross pension contributions do not exceed the amount of income you have taxed at 40%.

Example revisited
Sandy is a sole trader with pre-tax profits of £57,000. He has £6,730 of income taxed at 40% (£57,000 - £50,270 higher-rate threshold).

Sandy puts £15,000 into his pension. The taxman adds £3,750 of basic-rate relief. His gross contribution is £18,750 (£15,000/0.8).

His basic-rate band is increased by £18,750 which means his maximum higher-rate tax relief is:

£18,750 x 20% = £3,750

However, Sandy does not have £18,750 of income taxed at 40%, he only has £6,730. So the actual higher-rate relief he will receive is:

£6,730 x 20% = £1,346

Although his basic-rate band has been increased significantly, he doesn't have enough income to use it! Sandy is only obtaining higher-rate tax relief on £6,730 worth of pension contributions. In total he enjoys just 27% tax relief:

(£3,750 + £1,346) / £18,750 = 27%

What can Sandy do if he wants to enjoy the maximum higher-rate relief? He can spread his contributions over several tax years.

If he wants to invest £15,000 (£18,750 gross) and if we assume he has around £6,730 of income per year taxed at 40%, this means he could consider spreading his pension contributions over three tax years:

	Gross	**Cash contribution**
Year 1	£6,730	£5,384
Year 2	£6,730	£5,384
Year 3	£5,290	£4,232

Table 1
Maximising Higher-Rate Tax Relief:
Maximum Pension Contributions 2026/27

Taxable Income £	Maximum Gross Contribution £	Maximum Cash Contribution £
50,270	0	0
55,000	4,730	3,784
60,000	9,730	7,784
65,000	14,730	11,784
70,000	19,730	15,784
75,000	24,730	19,784
80,000	29,730	23,784
85,000	34,730	27,784
90,000	39,730	31,784
95,000	44,730	35,784
100,000	49,730	39,784

Rule of Thumb

If maximising tax relief is your priority, the maximum amount you should contribute to a pension in the current tax year is:

Your taxable income minus *£50,270*

This is your maximum *gross* pension contribution. Multiply this number by 0.8 to obtain the maximum amount you can actually invest (your net cash contribution).

Table 1 shows the maximum pension contribution you can make, depending on your income, if maximising higher-rate tax relief is your priority.

For example, someone with taxable income of £80,000 should make a cash contribution of no more than £23,784 this year.

This will result in a gross contribution of £29,730, which is well below the maximum permitted gross contribution of £60,000.

More than 40% Tax Relief

If you have taxable income of more than £100,000 you can enjoy more than 40% tax relief on your pension contributions, possibly as much as 60% tax relief.

So this chapter is mainly aimed at those earning more than £50,270 but less than £100,000. We'll return to high earners in Chapter 21.

Big Contributions Close to Retirement

When you are close to retirement it may be worth making pension contributions that are larger than normal, even if you only enjoy basic-rate tax relief.

This is because it is possible to withdraw all the extra money you contribute immediately after you retire and 25% will be tax free. (I'm assuming your existing pension savings do not already use up your maximum tax-free lump sum of £268,275.)

We'll take a look at the potential tax savings in Chapter 11.

Higher-Rate Taxpayers in Scotland

As we saw in Chapter 1, Scotland has more income tax bands than the rest of the UK. One of the biggest tax increases occurs when your income rises above £43,662. At this point you become a higher-rate taxpayer and your income tax rate jumps from 21% to 42%.

If you're a Scottish taxpayer, the maximum you should contribute to a pension if you want to enjoy *at least* 42% tax relief is:

Your taxable income <u>minus</u> *£43,662*

For example, a Scottish taxpayer who earns £50,000 can make a gross pension contribution of £6,338. This includes 20% basic-rate relief. The net cash contribution would be £5,070 (£6,338 x 0.8).

As a higher-rate taxpayer (paying 42% tax) an extra £1,394 of tax relief can then be claimed back (£6,338 x 22%).

Remember the Scottish Parliament can tax most types of income but NOT interest and dividends. So if you are a company owner in Scotland and pay yourself a small salary and the rest of your income comes in the shape of dividends, the relevant higher-rate threshold is the "Westminster" one – £50,270. (See Chapter 26 for more on how many company directors structure their pay.)

Example
Angus is a sole trader based in Scotland with taxable income of £50,000 in 2026/27. Angus can make a gross pension contribution of £6,338 (£50,000 - £43,662) with full higher-rate tax relief.

Douglas is a company director/shareholder based in Scotland with the same amount of taxable income (£50,000) but made up mostly of dividends. If Douglas makes a pension contribution of £6,338 he will not enjoy any higher-rate tax relief because he is not a higher-rate taxpayer (the UK, not Scottish, higher-rate threshold applies to his dividend income).

Advanced Rate Taxpayers in Scotland

Scottish taxpayers who earn between £75,000 and £100,000 now pay income tax at 45%. They can thus enjoy 45% tax relief on any pension contributions they make in this tax bracket.

For example, someone with earnings of £80,000 who makes an £8,000 gross pension contribution will enjoy 45% tax relief on the first £5,000 and 42% tax relief on the remaining £3,000.

The total tax relief is £3,510 which is 43.9%.

Chapter 5

How to Claim Higher-Rate Tax Relief

Scottish Widows once reported that up to a quarter of higher-rate taxpayers did not claim all the tax relief they were entitled to.

Many taxpayers believe incorrectly that all of their pension tax relief is automatically credited to their pension pot.

Those who do NOT have to claim higher-rate tax relief are members of so-called 'net pay' arrangements. These include many traditional occupational pension schemes. Your pension contributions are paid out of your salary before tax is deducted, so full 40% tax relief is effectively granted immediately.

Those who do have to claim higher-rate tax relief are members of so-called 'relief at source' arrangements. These include personal pensions, SIPPs and some workplace pensions.

With these arrangements the contributions are made out of your after-tax pay. The pension company then has to claim basic-rate tax relief from HMRC and you have to claim higher-rate tax relief.

Gross vs Net Contributions

Another mistake made by higher-rate taxpayers when completing tax returns is entering net cash pension contributions (the amount they actually pay in), instead of their gross contributions (which include the taxman's basic-rate tax relief top up).

Page 4 of your tax return is for 'Tax reliefs'. Box 1 asks for:

Payments to registered pension schemes where basic rate tax relief will be claimed by your pension provider (called 'relief at source'). Enter the payments and basic rate tax

If you personally pay £3,000 into your pension and insert this number on your tax return, the taxman will give you up to £600 of higher-rate tax relief: £3,000 x 20% = £600.

But if you enter the correct amount, which is £3,750 (£3,000/0.8), the taxman will give you up to £750 of higher-rate tax relief:

£3,750 x 20% = £750

Do not include employer pension contributions.

In Box 1.1 you can put any one-off contributions that are included in Box 1 that you do not intend to repeat in the current tax year. This will help ensure that HMRC gets your tax code right for the current tax year if you have one (otherwise you may end up paying too little tax).

Backdated Claims

If you have not claimed your higher-rate tax relief, the good news is you can make a backdated claim to HMRC.

You can claim for the previous four tax years. So, you could claim as far back as the 2022/2023 tax year before 5th April 2027. Rebates can run to thousands of pounds.

If you have not completed a tax return for any of the years in question you can claim back tax relief using HMRC's online tool:

www.gov.uk/guidance/claim-tax-relief-on-your-private-pension-payments

If you have completed a tax return you will have to write to HMRC or perhaps speak to your accountant.

How to Claim Higher-Rate Tax Relief

If you complete a self-assessment tax return you claim higher-rate tax relief (or additional-rate relief) when you submit your tax return.

Those who are not in self assessment can contact HMRC to claim the extra tax relief. Tax relief is given through your PAYE tax code. This allows tax relief to be provided immediately because less tax will be deducted from your salary each month. Claims can be made using HMRC's online service:

www.gov.uk/guidance/claim-tax-relief-on-your-private-pension-payments

You will need to provide evidence from the pension provider or your employer detailing the amount of pension contributions made.

Chapter 6

Will Higher-Rate Tax Relief Be Scrapped?

For many years now there have been fears the Government will take away the extra tax relief enjoyed by higher-rate taxpayers (and additional-rate taxpayers) on their pension contributions.

Up until recently this was done *indirectly* by reducing the annual allowance from £255,000 to £40,000 and freezing it for many years. A clamp down on high earners came into effect in 2016 with the introduction of the tapered annual allowance (see Chapter 21).

David Cameron's government consulted on whether to completely reform pension tax relief and an announcement was expected in the March 2016 Budget. However, in that Budget speech Chancellor George Osborne stated that "it was clear there is no consensus" and pension tax relief was left unchanged. Apparently the decision to leave pension tax relief alone was made so as to not antagonize voters before the EU referendum!

A little bit later there were newspaper reports that George Osborne's successor, Philip Hammond, had made cutting pension tax relief a priority. However, in July 2017, while speaking to the Association of British Insurers, Secretary of State for Work and Pensions David Gauke said he did not expect any fundamental changes to pension tax relief in the near future.

The pensions industry took comfort from this comment but then in February 2020 there was fresh speculation that former Chancellor Sajid Javid was considering cutting higher-rate tax relief. He resigned before he could cause any damage and was replaced as Chancellor by Rishi Sunak.

In his March 2020 Budget speech Rishi Sunak made no mention of higher-rate tax relief and instead increased the income thresholds where the tapered annual allowance applies (see Chapter 21). This has helped high income earners benefit from the full annual allowance (currently £60,000), without any reduction.

Before the March 2021 Budget there were, once again, rumours doing the rounds that the Government would scrap higher-rate tax relief or launch some sort of consultation. To everyone's relief no such announcement was made.

In June 2021 the *Telegraph* newspaper reported that the Government was considering replacing higher-rate tax relief with a flat rate of tax relief for everyone (possibly around 30%), with an announcement expected in the 2021 Autumn Statement. Once again no such announcement was made.

The rumours were again circulating ahead of the November 2022 Autumn Statement with one tabloid newspaper boldly stating that: "Prime Minister Rishi Sunak and Chancellor Jeremy Hunt are lining up yet another pensions tax raid... Finally, it looks like it's going to happen, with Ministers preparing to cut relief for higher earners. It may be slashed from 40 percent or 45 percent to just 20 percent, in line with basic-rate tax relief".

And what did the Government do? Absolutely nothing.

In the March 2023 Budget there was some good news: Chancellor Jeremy Hunt surprised everyone by increasing the annual allowance from £40,000 to £60,000 and scrapping the lifetime allowance charge.

In the run up to the October 2024 Budget rumours were circulating yet again that the new Labour Chancellor Rachel Reeves would scrap higher-rate tax relief or make other changes, for example reduce the amount of tax-free cash that can be taken or impose national insurance on employer contributions. There was a huge sigh of relief when none of these came to pass, although she did announce that pensions will be subject to inheritance tax from 6th April 2027.

Similar rumours were doing the rounds before the November 2025 Budget and this time a change to pension tax relief was announced: From April 2029, only the first £2,000 of salary sacrifice pension contributions will be exempt from national insurance (see Chapter 24 for more information).

Fortunately, no changes were made to income tax relief on pension contributions and ordinary employer pension contributions will remain exempt from national insurance.

Will the income tax relief on pension contributions be reduced in the future? We at Taxcafe remain hopeful (but not confident) that there will be no major changes that reduce the attractiveness of making pension contributions.

If there is a further raid on pensions it could come in the form of a reduction in the £60,000 annual allowance or a flat-rate model could be introduced with everyone given tax relief at say 30%. Alternatively the Government could reduce the amount of tax-free cash you can take (currently £268,275).

It's important to remember that pensions are long-term savings vehicles, with contributions often made over many decades. It would be very brave to predict that the same level of tax relief will be available in five, 10 or 20 years' time.

The truth is nobody knows what will happen in the years ahead, although further changes do seem likely at some point.

For many years now pension companies have advised higher-rate and additional-rate taxpayers to make bigger pension contributions in case the extra tax relief is scrapped. To date all such predictions have been proved wrong. Nevertheless it is a concern that the pension tax reliefs seem to be continually on the Government's radar.

Many higher-rate and additional-rate taxpayers may feel they have nothing to lose by making bigger contributions with full 40% or 45% tax relief while this is still possible.

The ongoing saga around pension tax relief highlights the major drawback of this savings vehicle: almost every benefit can be taken away by politicians at the stroke of a pen.

They can change the tax reliefs, the age you can access your savings, restrict how you invest your savings and make withdrawals and increase the tax paid on the money you take out or leave to your family.

Part 2

Taking Money Out: The Pension Freedom Rules

Chapter 7

Introduction

Before Age 55

At present you generally cannot withdraw any money from your pension until you're 55. This is one of the major drawbacks. There are times in life when even financially conservative individuals may need to tap their retirement savings early.

Obvious examples would be to pay for a child's education or unforeseen family medical expenses. In the worst case scenario you may even need to access your savings early to avoid bankruptcy or home repossession. So if you're under 55 and want to make significant pension contributions you should make sure you have other resources to protect against:

- Unforeseen expenses, and an
- Unforeseen drop in income.

Although you cannot withdraw anything until you're 55, it's important to point out that the money can usually be invested as you please. These days many personal pensions plans, especially SIPPs, provide enormous investment flexibility.

Note too that 55 is the minimum age that normally applies to defined contribution pension schemes. Some defined benefit schemes impose a higher normal retirement age (typically between 60 and 65) if you want to receive a full pension.

Early Access on Health Grounds

Pension savers of any age who suffer from "serious ill health" (including those under age 55) can apply to their pension provider to have their uncrystallised pension savings paid out as a lump sum.

Serious ill health means less than 12 months to live, as certified by a registered medical practitioner. Uncrystallised pension savings are those that haven't been accessed yet.

All uncrystallised funds in the pension arrangement must be paid out. A partial withdrawal cannot be made (although it may be possible to make a partial transfer of the fund to another pension provider and achieve the same result).

Serious ill health lump sums are free from income tax if the person is under age 75 and has enough of their Lump Sum and Death Benefit Allowance remaining (see Chapter 10). Any amount over the allowance is subject to income tax.

This allowance is typically £1,073,100 but is reduced by any tax-free lump sums already taken.

If the person is 75 or older the full serious ill health lump sum will be subject to income tax, which means there is probably nothing to be gained from applying for one – money can simply be withdrawn from the pension in the normal way.

Even if the individual is under 75, taking a tax-free serious ill-health lump sum may not always be the best option, unless there is an immediate need for cash. If the individual is under age 75 when they die, their beneficiaries will also be able to withdraw money from the inherited pension pot free from income tax.

Whether the money is inside or outside a pension arrangement when the individual dies it seems likely it will be potentially subject to inheritance tax from 6th April 2027.

Ill Health

Pension savings can also be accessed at any age if the individual suffers from "ill health". This means the individual is medically incapable of carrying on their *current* occupation. Some scheme rules are stricter and may state that you have to be incapable of carrying on *any* occupation.

The tax treatment is the same as when benefits are accessed at normal retirement age: up to 25% can be taken as a tax-free lump sum, with anything else taxed as income.

Future Changes to the Minimum Pension Age

On 6th April 2028 the minimum age at which most people can access their private pensions will increase from 55 to 57, when the state pension age is increased to 67.

The practical implications are as follows:

- **Born on or before 6th April 1971** – you won't be affected because you'll already be 57 on 6th April 2028.

- **Born after 5th April 1973** – you will have to wait until you're 57 to withdraw any money from your pension.

- **Born after 6th April 1971 but before 6th April 1973** – you will turn 55 before 6th April 2028 and will have a window from your 55th birthday until 5th April 2028 to withdraw money. However, when 6th April 2028 comes around you won't be 57 yet. Thus if you haven't made any pension withdrawals you will have to wait until your 57th birthday before any money can be taken out.

Those who fall under the third bullet point are in the most confusing position. At the time of writing it was not clear how those who access some but not all of their pension savings before 6th April 2028 will be treated from that date forward.

For example, if you withdraw just some of your tax-free cash will you be prevented from taking any more until you reach age 57?

We hope this will not be the case and the Government has stated that guidance on transitional arrangements will be provided soon.

The cliff edge nature of the increase from age 55 to 57 also seems badly thought out and cruel. If you were born on 5th April 1973 you will turn 55 on 5th April 2028 and can, in theory, withdraw money from your pension on that day. However, if you are unable to do so for various practical reasons (or because like any normal person you are celebrating your birthday!), you will wake up on the 6th of April and find that you cannot withdraw any money for a further two years.

This is the most extreme example but a similar cliff edge is faced by many other people who were born in the April 1971 to 1973 window.

The increase in the minimum pension age from 55 to 57 was put into legislation as part of the Finance Act 2022.

Pension schemes for the armed forces, police and firefighters are not affected.

The legislation also introduces a "protected pension age". Members of registered pension schemes (occupational or non-occupational) who have an existing right under the scheme's rules to take pension benefits at age 55 will be protected from the increase to 57 in 2028. Most SIPPs and personal pensions do not allow for this.

The right to take benefits at 55 must have been in the scheme's rules as of 11th February 2021. New members of such schemes will also be protected as long as they joined before 4th November 2021.

Members of pension schemes who do not have such a right will see their minimum pension age increase to 57 on 6th April 2028.

Further Increases in the Pension Age

The state pension age is legislated to increase over the next couple of decades. The Government's position is that it is, in principle, appropriate for the age at which people can access their private pensions to remain around 10 years below the state pension age. However, an automatic link has not been created yet.

An increase to the state pension age from 67 to 68 is pencilled in for the mid 2040s but an earlier increase is very likely, possibly at some point during the 2030s.

Pension Freedom

When you turn 55 (or 57 from 2028) you can start tapping your pension. You can take as much money as you like, whenever you like.

You can withdraw the whole lot in one go or leave your entire pension pot untouched and give it to your family when you die (see Chapter 10).

Most people will probably do something in between these two extremes. For example, when you're 55 or 57 you could take your tax-free lump sum and leave the rest of your savings to grow tax free until you retire and then start withdrawing income gradually.

Saving income tax will be a key consideration (see Chapter 11).

Under the pension freedom rules you can use one or more of the following products to access your pension:

- Flexi-access drawdown
- Uncrystallised funds pension lump sum (UFPLS)
- Lifetime annuity

Flexi-access drawdown lets you take your entire tax-free lump sum in one go and place your remaining savings into drawdown, where the money can be accessed as and when you like.

Taking an uncrystallised funds pension lump sum allows you to take your tax-free lump sum in stages instead of in one go. Like drawdown, you can make withdrawals as and when you like but one quarter of every withdrawal will be tax free with the remainder taxed as income.

Annuities were out of favour when interest rates were low. Low interest rates meant low levels of income for anyone who purchased one. Apparently annuities are coming back into fashion now that interest rates have increased. They've also been unpopular because the life insurance company generally confiscates your pension savings when you die or your spouse dies. Despite their drawbacks, annuities provide a guaranteed "risk-free" income for life, unlike drawdown and UFPLS.

The various income options are discussed further in Chapter 8.

Defined Benefit Pensions

The pension freedom reforms apply to "defined contribution" pensions only: personal pensions and SIPPs and many occupational pension schemes in the private sector.

They're not available to members of defined benefit schemes (also known as final salary pension schemes). Members of these schemes cannot withdraw money as and when they like.

However, if you belong to a final salary scheme it may be possible to transfer to a defined contribution scheme (such as a SIPP) and collect a large cash lump sum. The value of final salary transfers often runs to hundreds of thousands of pounds.

Members of unfunded public sector pension schemes (i.e. teachers, NHS employees and civil servants) are not able to transfer to a defined contribution scheme and access their pension as a lump sum. Unfunded pension schemes are ones that don't have any assets – they rely on taxpayers to keep up the pension payments.

Members of funded public sector schemes (e.g. the local government one) can transfer to a defined contribution scheme.

Transferring to a personal pension may allow you to access your pension savings more flexibly and leave surplus funds to your children (after paying any inheritance tax that may be due under the proposed change from 6th April 2027).

However, pension transfers are also highly controversial, which is why impartial professional advice is necessary.

Many pension experts advise against transferring from a "gold-plated" final salary scheme, which offers a guaranteed income for life, to a "crummy" personal pension, where your retirement income will depend on how well your investments perform. Members of final salary schemes do not have to worry about the ups and downs of the stock market!

Research by pension consultancy XPS showed that people who transfer out of final salary schemes were paying record annual fees in their new schemes (1.9% per year on average). The difference between the cheapest and most expensive pension schemes amounted to an additional £8,500 per year in charges.

Income Tax on Pension Withdrawals

Although you can take up to one quarter of your pension savings as a tax-free lump sum (see Chapter 3), you have to pay income tax on everything else you withdraw, *including your original contributions*.

That's a bit like putting £100 in a bank account and paying £20 or maybe £40 tax when you withdraw the money a year later. Of course, this doesn't happen when you withdraw money from your bank account – at most you will pay tax on your interest.

So while pensions offer several tax concessions, there is a tax sting at the end.

Thus, the sixty-four-thousand dollar question is this:

Do the tax benefits – tax relief on contributions and tax-free investment growth – outweigh the drawback of taxed withdrawals?

In most cases the answer is "Yes". This is because most people will probably pay basic-rate tax (currently 20%) on the money they take out but will enjoy at least 40% tax relief when they put their money in, if they are higher-rate taxpayers.

Furthermore, some of the money you take out will be tax free, including your tax-free lump sum and any withdrawals that are covered by your income tax personal allowance.

This is why even basic-rate taxpayers will usually also end up better off with a pension. Although they only enjoy basic-rate tax relief when they put their money in, a significant chunk of the money they take out could be tax free.

But *exactly* how much better off are you likely to be with a pension? The benefits surely have to be significant to justify putting your money into a locked box until you are 55 or older.

One way to answer this question is to compare two investors: one putting money into a pension and the other putting money into a different tax shelter, an ISA, and see who ends up better off at the end of the day. We do this in Chapter 15.

Like pensions, money in ISAs grows tax free. However, unlike pensions, ISAs do not offer any upfront tax relief but all your withdrawals are tax free and your money is not tied up until age 55 or later – you can withdraw it whenever you like.

However, the problem with using ISAs as retirement saving vehicles is they give you tax relief when you may need it least. It's usually better to have 40% tax relief when you put your money in, as you do with pensions if you're a higher-rate taxpayer, rather than 20% tax relief when you take it out, as you effectively do with ISAs if you're a basic-rate taxpayer when you retire.

If you're under 40 you can also invest in a Lifetime ISA. These arguably offer the best of both worlds: upfront tax relief (in the shape of a Government bonus) and tax-free withdrawals. We also compare Lifetime ISAs and pensions in Chapter 15.

Pension Advice

The Pensions Advice Allowance allows you to withdraw £500 tax free from your pension pot on three occasions (i.e. three separate tax years) to pay for pensions and retirement advice. The allowance is available at any age and to members of defined contribution pension schemes (not final salary pension schemes).

However, it's important to point out that very few pension providers offer this facility.

Chapter 8

Flexi-Access Drawdown & UFPLS

If you want to make use of the flexible regime for pension withdrawals you have two choices:

- Flexi-access drawdown
- Uncrystallised funds pension lump sum (UFPLS)

Some pension providers will only offer very limited options so you may have to shop around and, in some cases, it may even be necessary to transfer your pension to another provider.

Flexi-Access Drawdown

When you reach pension age (currently 55) you can move some or all of your pension savings into flexi-access drawdown.

Up to one quarter (25%) can be taken as a tax-free cash lump sum and only flexi-access drawdown allows you to take your tax-free lump sum on its own without any additional taxable income (for example, if you want to withdraw some cash to pay down your mortgage before you stop working).

The remaining 75% continues to grow tax free in your drawdown account until you start making withdrawals. You can withdraw as much income as you like whenever you like. All withdrawals from your drawdown account will be fully taxed.

If at any point you decide you want a more secure income for the rest of your life, you can use some or all of your remaining drawdown funds to buy an annuity.

Remember the maximum tax-free cash you can withdraw from your pension is capped at £268,275 for most people (see Chapter 3).

Phased Drawdown

If you don't want to take your entire tax-free lump sum in one go, you can use something called phased drawdown. For example, you may wish to withdraw a small tax-free lump sum to buy a car or for home improvements.

Phased drawdown may also appeal to those who are semi-retired. It allows you to make regular tax-free withdrawals to supplement your income before you are fully retired.

Then when you stop working completely (and your tax rate is hopefully lower) you can start withdrawing money from the taxable portion of your pension pot.

By not withdrawing your entire tax-free lump sum in one go, the money can continue to grow tax free inside your pension. As a result you may end up with more tax-free cash overall.

Example
Stacey is 58 and still working and has a SIPP worth £300,000. She is currently entitled to take out £75,000 (25%) as tax-free cash but decides to take just £10,000.

Using flexi-access drawdown she crystallises £40,000 of her SIPP. £10,000 (25%) is paid out to her as tax-free cash. The remaining £30,000 is placed in a separate drawdown account.

She can withdraw the money in the drawdown account whenever she likes but the withdrawals will be subject to income tax (possibly at 40% or more if she is still working).

Stacey now has two pension accounts: her original SIPP which is now worth £260,000 (£300,000 - £40,000) and a drawdown account worth £30,000. The money in both accounts will continue growing tax free and she can choose how each account is invested.

Let's assume a couple of years later her original SIPP has grown from £260,000 to £315,000 and her drawdown account has grown from £30,000 to £36,000. She is now entitled to take £78,750 (£315,000 x 25%) as tax-free cash but decides to take just £10,000 again.

She crystallises a further £40,000 of her SIPP savings with £10,000 paid out as tax-free cash and the remaining £30,000 placed in her drawdown account, along with the £36,000 that is already there.

Her original SIPP is now worth £275,000 (£315,000 - £40,000) and her drawdown account is worth £66,000 (£30,000 + £36,000).

Stacey can keep doing this, as often as she likes, until she has crystallised all of her original SIPP savings and moved the balance (the amount remaining after tax-free cash has been paid out) into her drawdown account.

For example, let's assume three years later her original SIPP has grown from £275,000 to £366,000 and her drawdown account has grown from £66,000 to £88,000. She can now take up to £91,500 of her SIPP savings as tax-free cash (£366,000 x 25%).

If she does this the remaining £274,500 will be placed in her drawdown account (£366,000 - £91,500), along with the £88,000 that is already there.

She will then be left with a drawdown account worth £362,500 (£274,500 + £88,000) from which all future withdrawals will be subject to income tax.

Alternatively she can continue taking smaller amounts of tax-free cash, as often as she likes, until she has crystallised all of her original SIPP savings. She can also withdraw money from her drawdown account whenever she likes but subject to income tax.

The overall amount of tax-free she can take is restricted to the £268,275 Lump Sum Allowance (see Chapter 3). Stacey is well within this limit.

Withdrawing Tax-Free Cash in Practice

These days it is extremely easy to withdraw tax-free cash from your pension and the whole process can be completed quickly online.

You may have to sell some of your pension investments, so that there is enough cash to pay the tax-free lump sum into your bank account. You may also have to tell your pension provider which of your remaining investments you wish to transfer from your original pension to your drawdown account – the remaining 75% of the amount crystallised.

Uncrystallised Funds Pension Lump Sum (UFPLS)

The pension freedom reforms were clearly made in a hurry. How else can you explain calling something an "uncrystallised funds pension lump sum", with the unwieldy acronym UFPLS?

With UFPLS you can take your entire pension pot as a lump sum in one go, or take a series of smaller lump sums. Each lump sum will have a 25% tax-free element, with the rest taxed as income.

As with flexi-access drawdown, the total amount of tax-free cash is capped at £268,275 for most people.

UFPLS may appeal to those who don't need all their tax-free cash immediately. Instead it can continue to grow tax free. Note, however, that a similar result can be achieved with flexi-access drawdown by using phased drawdown (if your pension provider offers it) and crystallising just a portion of your retirement savings.

Example

Zach has a £100,000 pension pot. He withdraws £20,000 using UFPLS, leaving £80,000 untouched. £5,000 of the UFPLS is tax-free cash, the remaining £15,000 is taxable. If we assume Zach has other income and is a basic-rate taxpayer he will pay 20% tax: £3,000. Zach can continue to use UFPLS to take lump sums as and when he needs. He can also move his remaining pension pot into flexi-access drawdown or, if he wants a secure income for the rest of his life with no investment risk, he can use his remaining funds to buy an annuity.

With UFPLS you have to take tax-free cash and taxable income at the same time – every withdrawal will consist of 25% tax-free cash and 75% taxable income.

Flexi-access drawdown is therefore more flexible than UFPLS because it lets you take tax-free cash without having to take any taxable income. This may be more appealing if you want to withdraw cash while you are still working and paying 40% or 45% tax. You can postpone withdrawing taxable income until you retire and start paying tax at perhaps 20%, if you are a basic-rate taxpayer when you retire.

The Money Purchase Annual Allowance (MPAA)

When you start withdrawing *income* from your pension pot, over and above your tax-free lump sum, your ability to make future pension contributions could be restricted.

Instead of being able to contribute £60,000 per year, you may only be able to contribute £10,000 per year. This is what's known as the money purchase annual allowance (MPAA).

The money purchase annual allowance used to be £4,000 but was increased to £10,000 on 6th April 2023.

In fact, this was the only pension change announced in the March 2023 Budget that benefited "regular" pension savers.

The other changes that were announced (the scrapping of the lifetime allowance, the increase in the annual allowance from £40,000 to £60,000 and changes to the tapered annual allowance – see Chapter 21) were all welcome but mainly benefit high income earners and more wealthy pension savers.

Thanks to the increase in the money purchase annual allowance some pension savers may feel less wary of withdrawing income from their pensions (for example if they're experiencing financial hardship), especially if they've already built up a significant pension pot and are close to retirement.

Nevertheless, although being able to contribute £10,000 per year is a lot better than being able to contribute just £4,000, the money purchase annual allowance still makes it harder for those who have withdrawn income from their pensions to replenish their retirement savings.

So it's important to make the point that you should be extremely wary of withdrawing taxable income from your pension pot if you intend to keep making pension contributions in the future.

Note that £10,000 is the maximum *gross* pension contribution you would be able to make. The maximum cash you could invest personally would be £8,000. The taxman would add £2,000 of basic-rate tax relief to produce a gross pension contribution of £10,000.

Note too that if you are subject to the money purchase annual allowance you also cannot carry forward any unused allowance from the three previous tax years.

If you use flexi-access drawdown and take your 25% tax-free lump but do not withdraw any additional taxable income, you get to keep your £60,000 annual allowance – you can keep making pension contributions just like anyone else.

However, as soon as you take any income from your drawdown plan the money purchase annual allowance will apply.

With uncrystallised funds pension lump sums (UFPLS) the money purchase annual allowance applies once you start making any pension withdrawals. In other words, as soon as you start withdrawing money using UFPLS your pension contributions could be restricted to £10,000 per year.

Thus, flexi-access drawdown may be more suitable for those who want to keep making significant pension contributions. You can withdraw some or all of your tax-free cash and keep making pension contributions of up to £60,000 per year and use your unused annual allowance from the previous three tax years.

The money purchase annual allowance was introduced to reduce pension recycling – taking income out of a pension and using it to make fresh contributions with tax relief.

It's also designed to prevent those aged 55 and over replacing their regular taxed salaries with employer pension contributions, 25% of which would perhaps be withdrawn tax free immediately.

Note that additional rules prevent tax-free lump sums being recycled (see Chapter 9).

The MPAA only applies to money purchase pension contributions (e.g. those paid into personal pensions and SIPPs). It does not restrict contributions to defined benefit pension schemes (final salary schemes).

In other words, your annual allowance for funding a defined benefit scheme will generally still be £60,000, less any money purchase contributions within the £10,000 limit.

The money purchase annual allowance also isn't triggered if:

- You use your pension savings to buy a standard lifetime annuity
- You are using capped drawdown (the old type of drawdown that is no longer available to new retirees) and do not withdraw income above the maximum income limit
- You cash in a small pension pot. You can take up to three pension pots worth up to £10,000 each (an unlimited number from occupational pension schemes)

Tax Overpayment Issues

When you withdraw income from your pension, the pension provider will deduct income tax before paying you.

When you make the first such withdrawal it is common for tax to be deducted using an 'emergency' tax code. This will often happen if you cannot provide a valid P45 to your pension company, following your withdrawal from employment.

In many cases applying an emergency tax code to the first payment will mean that far too much tax is deducted (often thousands of pounds too much) and you will be due a repayment.

For example, if you make a one-off income withdrawal of £10,000 at the start of the tax year, you could be taxed as if your pension income will be £10,000 *every month* – £120,000 for the year.

HMRC recently announced that, from April 2025, they have improved how tax code information is used for those new to receiving private pension income, so they pay the right amount of tax faster: *"We will automatically update the tax code for customers who are on a temporary tax code and would benefit from being on a cumulative code — this means they'll avoid an overpayment or underpayment at the end of the year."*

These changes should benefit those who take a regular monthly income from their pension. There should be a faster correction process with HMRC swiftly adjusting tax codes so that the correct amount of tax is deducted sooner than in the past. Any initial tax overpayment should be refunded via your ongoing pension withdrawals.

However, HMRC's new approach does not eliminate the application of emergency tax codes to initial pension withdrawals. Instead, HMRC will simply issue the correct tax code quicker than before. Tax overpayments may still be made before the correct adjustments are made.

Thus the changes may be less useful to those who make a single ad hoc pension withdrawal because the first such withdrawal will likely remain overtaxed. Some commentators advise savers planning to make a single withdrawal to make a small, notional withdrawal first. This should mean HMRC is able to apply the correct tax code to the second, larger withdrawal.

If you make a single withdrawal and are overtaxed you may need to complete one of three forms if you want to receive a refund quickly (within 30 days apparently):

- **Form P55** - If you decide to make a single withdrawal that does not empty your pension pot, and do not plan on making further withdrawals during the tax year

- **Form P50Z** - If you empty your pension pot and have no other PAYE or pension income (other than your state pension).

- **Form P53Z** - If you empty your pension pot and still have employment income or pension income

Chapter 9

The Pension Recycling Rules

When you start withdrawing income from a flexi-access drawdown account or make any withdrawal using UFPLS, you will be subject to the money purchase annual allowance.

This may limit your future money purchase pension contributions to £10,000 per year and prohibit you from carrying forward any unused annual allowance from the three previous tax years.

If you use flexi-access drawdown and withdraw your tax-free lump sum only (with no additional income) you can continue making pension contributions of up to £60,000 per year (if you have sufficient earnings) and use any unused annual allowance from the previous three tax years.

However, if you use your tax-free lump sum to make fresh pension contributions, you have to be wary of HMRC's recycling rules. These are designed to prevent tax-free cash being reinvested in a pension and enjoying a second round of tax relief.

Example
Toby is 59, still working and a higher-rate taxpayer. Over the last 10 years he has been making pension contributions of £6,000 per year. Using flexi-access drawdown he withdraws £10,000 of tax-free cash in order to reinvest it in a pension. The taxman adds £2,500 of basic-rate tax relief, giving him a total gross pension contribution of £12,500. Furthermore, when he submits his tax return he receives higher-rate tax relief of £2,500.

Unfortunately for Toby his pension contribution may fall foul of HMRC's recycling rules which are designed to prevent you making larger than normal pension contributions because you have received a tax-free lump sum.

The recycling rules can even apply if you make bigger than normal pension contributions *before* you withdraw tax-free cash.

If the recycling rules apply, your tax-free lump sum will be treated as an unauthorised payment, resulting in a tax charge of up to 70%.

The recycling rules apply when ALL of the following conditions are met:

- You receive a pension commencement lump sum (tax-free lump sum)
- The tax-free cash, including any tax-free cash taken in the previous 12 months, exceeds £7,500
- Because you took tax-free cash your pension contributions are significantly larger than they otherwise would be
- The additional contributions are more than 30% of the tax-free cash
- The recycling was pre-planned

Point 2 means that small amounts of recycling effectively fall under the radar.

Example
Using phased drawdown Justine takes a tax-free lump sum of £7,000 and immediately invests all of it in a pension plan, producing a gross pension contribution of £8,750 after basic-rate tax relief is added. She hasn't received any other tax-free cash in the previous 12 months so the pension contribution does not fall foul of the recycling rules, even though the recycling was pre-planned.

Looking at point 3, for the recycling rules to apply there must be a significant increase in your pension contributions. This includes contributions made by you and your employer.

HMRC will look at your contribution history to determine if there has been a significant increase. If you haven't made any pension contributions for a while, your last contribution may be adjusted for inflation to produce a current value for comparison purposes.

As a rule of thumb, HMRC may argue that your pension contributions have increased significantly if they are 30% larger than they would have been without the tax-free cash.

HMRC doesn't just look for big pension contributions in the tax year you receive tax-free cash. They will also look at contributions made in the two tax years before you received the cash and in the two tax years after you took the cash.

Example

Harvey is 60 and for the last five years has been making pension contributions of £10,000 per year. He takes a £40,000 tax-free lump sum from his pension and uses some of it to pay for a new kitchen and the rest to make a £25,000 pension contribution in the next tax year. Because his pension contribution is more than 30% larger than those made in recent years he may fall foul of the pension recycling rules.

The amount of additional contributions is measured on a cumulative basis which means you may be caught out even if you only make relatively small additional pension contributions after receiving your tax-free cash.

Example

Joan has been making pension contributions of £10,000 per year for the last 10 years. She takes £20,000 of tax-free cash from her pension and uses some of it to increase her pension contributions as follows:

	Contribution	***Increase***	***% Increase***
Current year	*£12,500*	*£2,500*	*25%*
One year later	*£12,500*	*£2,500*	*25%*
Two years later	*£12,500*	*£2,500*	*25%*
Cumulative increase		*£7,500*	*75%*

Joan's pension contributions have not increased by more than 30% in any single year but the cumulative increase is 75%. This is more than 30% which means there has been a significant increase.

Because the additional pension contributions were pre-planned she may have to pay £14,000 tax on the £20,000 tax-free lump sum.

Turning to point 4, you'll only be caught by the recycling rules if your additional contributions are more than 30% of your tax-free lump sum. In Joan's case her additional contributions were £7,500 and are more than 30% of her tax-free lump sum (£20,000 x 30% = £6,000).

However, if her additional contributions were less than £2,000 per year (less than £6,000 in total) this would presumably not count as pension recycling.

Point 5 is the most vague. The recycling must be pre-planned which means you must have intended to take your tax-free lump sum to make significantly greater pension contributions. If you decide to use your tax-free lump sum to significantly increase your pension contributions but make the contributions *before* receiving your tax-free lump sum this may also be treated as pre-planning (for example, if you use other savings or a loan to pay the contributions and then use your lump sum to replenish those savings or pay off the loan). Where, on the other hand, you take a lump sum and only later decide to use it to make bigger contributions, there is no pre-planning.

When the Recycling Rules Do Not Apply

The key is that the recycling rules apply when your pension contributions are significantly increased "because of" the tax-free lump sum.

There are other reasons why your pension contributions may increase significantly from year to year and they should not constitute recycling.

For example, let's say you increase your pension contributions from £10,000 to £15,000 in the year you take tax-free cash. Although your pension contributions have increased by more than 30% this may be because you've received a bonus or the profits of your business have increased or because you have more income taxed at 40% and want to maximise your higher-rate tax relief.

If you can demonstrate that, although your pension contributions have fluctuated, they are calculated on a consistent basis (e.g. as a percentage of your income) the recycling rules should not apply.

The recycling rules will also not apply if you make significantly larger pension contributions because you receive a cash windfall such as an inheritance.

Example

Sadie takes tax-free cash from her pension. A few months later her father dies leaving her a substantial inheritance. Because of the inheritance (and not because she received a pension lump sum), she decides to make larger than normal pension contributions. She invests the whole inheritance in her pension. These pension contributions will not constitute recycling because she did not pre-plan to use the pension lump sum to make significantly larger pension contributions.

In summary, it may be possible to trickle some of your tax-free lump sum back into a pension, providing the additional annual contributions are very small and made over many tax years. However, it's important to stress that this is high-risk tax planning because if you get it wrong the penalties are severe. Anyone thinking of making larger than normal pension contributions a couple of years before or after taking tax-free cash should probably seek professional advice.

Chapter 10

Leaving Your Pension Pot to Your Family

After you die your remaining pension savings can go to your family. The money can be left to one or a combination of people: your spouse or partner, your children or anyone else for that matter.

Your beneficiaries will not have to wait until they themselves reach the minimum pension age (currently 55) to access the money. They could take the money as a cash lump sum paid into their bank accounts or, alternatively, they can ask the pension company to set up 'beneficiary drawdown' accounts in their names. The money in these accounts will continue to grow tax free and can be withdrawn without limit as and when your beneficiaries need it.

At present the money left in your pension pot when you die typically falls outside your estate for inheritance tax (IHT) purposes. However, under current Government proposals, from 6th April 2027 pension savings will become subject to inheritance tax.

For the majority of this chapter we will assume that the reader dies *after* this date and his or her remaining pension savings are therefore exposed to inheritance tax.

Your beneficiaries may also have to pay *income tax* on any money they withdraw from the inherited pension pot, after any inheritance tax bill has been settled.

Note that full details of how inheritance tax will be applied to pensions have not been finalised. Draft legislation has been published but various expert commentators argue that parts of it are unworkable in their current form. Thus it's possible there will be further changes before the draft legislation becomes law.

However, the key point is that it is very unlikely that there will be a complete Government u-turn: pensions will, in all likelihood, become subject to inheritance tax from 6th April 2027.

Inheritance Tax

The Current Position

Your pension savings are typically held in trust outside your estate and are thus free from inheritance tax in most cases.

The administrator of the pension scheme normally has discretion over who receives the money when you die, although they will be guided by your wishes, which can be stated by completing an expression of wish form. Because these forms are usually not legally binding (although rarely ignored), your pension savings do not form part of your estate for inheritance tax purposes.

Note, not all pensions escape inheritance tax at present. Some schemes are 'non-discretionary' (the manager of the scheme has no discretion when it comes to awarding benefits and must follow the member's instructions) and are treated as part of the estate for inheritance tax purposes.

An inheritance tax charge may also arise at present if you make unusually large pension contributions because you are in ill health and then die within two years. Someone in ill health may do this to try and take some of their assets out of the inheritance tax net.

An inheritance tax charge may also arise in certain circumstances if you transfer from one pension scheme to another while in ill health and die within two years of making the transfer. For example, someone in ill health may transfer out of a final salary scheme, with limited death benefits, to a personal pension which allows their pension savings to pass to their children.

Proposed Changes

From 6th April 2027, when a pension scheme member dies their remaining pension savings will become part of their estate for inheritance tax purposes.

The current distinction between discretionary and non-discretionary schemes will be removed.

As with other assets, the spouse exemption will apply to pension savings. In other words, if your pension savings are left to your spouse or civil partner when you die there will be no inheritance tax payable on this asset.

If your pension savings are left to someone else (for example an unmarried partner or your children), inheritance tax may be payable. However, some of your £325,000 nil rate band will typically be available to reduce the amount of tax payable.

If you leave some or all of your assets (including your pension) to your spouse, their nil rate band could be as much as £650,000 when they themselves die.

Thanks to the nil rate band the effective rate of inheritance tax payable on inherited pensions is likely to be less than the 40% headline rate.

Exemptions from IHT

Apart from the exemption for pension savings left to spouses, other exemptions from inheritance tax include:

- Charity lump sum death benefits, where the charity is a nominated beneficiary and you have no dependants.
- Dependants' scheme pensions and death-in-service benefits
- Joint life annuities – the survivor's rights are considered separate from the deceased's rights and therefore outside the deceased's estate for inheritance tax purposes.

How Inheritance Tax Will Be Administered

In a change from what was originally proposed, personal representatives (the executors where the deceased has left a will) will be responsible for reporting and paying any inheritance tax due, not the pension scheme administrator. However, pension scheme administrators will have new duties to support personal representatives in paying inheritance tax.

Being caught in the inheritance tax net means passing on pensions will become more complicated and take much longer than before.
The process is expected to work as follows:

- The personal representatives will notify the pension administrator of the death and let them know if there is a surviving spouse.
- The pension administrator will have four weeks to let the personal representatives know the value of the pension pot. The pension administrator will determine how the pension savings are to be distributed (exercising their discretion where required) and inform the personal representatives.

- Once the personal representatives know the value of the pension pot and how it is to be divided between exempt beneficiaries (for example, a surviving spouse) and non-exempt beneficiaries (typically children or grandchildren), they can work out how much inheritance tax is payable.

- Where there is no inheritance tax payable, the pension administrator can distribute the funds to the beneficiaries.

- If inheritance tax is due, the personal representatives will inform the pension beneficiaries and the pension administrator of the amount of tax due.

In the November 2025 Budget it was announced that, if the personal representatives expect inheritance tax to be payable on the pension, in some circumstances they will be able to direct the pension scheme administrator to withhold up to 50% of the pension benefits for up to 15 months and pay the inheritance tax straight to HMRC.

Inheritance tax will be payable in one of three ways:

- The personal representatives can pay the inheritance tax bill in full out of the general estate. If the pension beneficiaries are not the same people as the beneficiaries of the general estate, the personal representatives will then be able to reclaim the inheritance tax arising on the pension fund from the pension beneficiaries.

- The pension beneficiaries or personal representatives can ask the pension administrator to pay the inheritance tax arising on the pension fund directly out of the inherited pension. The pension administrator will generally be obliged to do this if the tax bill is £1,000 or more. It will not be possible to get the pension administrator to pay the inheritance tax due on other assets in the estate out of the pension: only the inheritance tax arising on the pension fund itself can be settled this way.

- The pension beneficiaries can withdraw their pension savings and settle their inheritance tax bills directly. If they have to pay income tax on these withdrawals, it will be possible to claim an income tax exemption on an amount equal to the amount of inheritance tax payable. This is to protect the beneficiaries from having to pay income tax on withdrawals made purely to settle an inheritance tax bill.

Preventing Double Taxation

Getting the pension administrator to settle the inheritance tax bill directly from the pension fund is arguably the simplest option.

If the personal representatives pay the pension's inheritance tax bill out of the estate's other assets there would be a danger of double taxation on the pension. This is because the general estate would end up smaller than otherwise and the pension pot would end up bigger than otherwise. If the beneficiaries then had to pay income tax on the excess money in the pension when they withdrew it, they would effectively end up paying income tax on the pension pot's inheritance tax bill.

Fortunately, a special income tax exemption is being put in place to prevent this from happening. The following example illustrates how we think this may work:

Example

Mary dies in June 2027 at age 85 with a pension pot worth £500,000. Her son James is the nominated beneficiary and has the pension placed into a drawdown account. Let's say inheritance tax of £125,000 is due on the pension, which Mary's personal representatives paid out of her general estate. Later in 2027/28 James withdraws £40,000 from the inherited pension which is subject to income tax.

James will be entitled to an income tax exemption equal to the lesser of:

- *£125,000 (total IHT paid on pension)*
- *£40,000 (taxable pension income)*

James can deduct £40,000 from his taxable income in 2027/28 which means he pays no income tax on the pension withdrawal. The remaining £85,000 of exemption in respect of the inheritance tax paid can be carried forward and used in future tax years. Once James has withdrawn £125,000 from the inherited pension, income tax will be payable on any further withdrawals.

As stated earlier, getting the pension administrator to settle the inheritance tax bill directly from the pension fund may be the simplest option.

Note that it will not be possible to get the pension administrator to pay the inheritance tax due on other assets in the estate – only the pension's own inheritance bill can be settled this way.

For example, if a surviving child has to withdraw money from an inherited pension to settle the inheritance tax due on a holiday home they wish to keep in the family rather than sell, the pension withdrawals will be subject to income tax if the deceased parent was 75 or older (the income tax treatment of inherited pensions is examined in more detail later in this chapter).

Such withdrawals would not qualify for the special income tax exemption discussed above.

A reasonably large pension withdrawal in these circumstances could be taxed at between 40% and 60%, depending on how much other income the surviving child has.

Of course, there are alternatives to making a big heavily taxed pension withdrawal. For example, the surviving child could perhaps borrow money to settle the inheritance tax bill on the property or elect to pay the tax in 10 yearly instalments (although there is a hefty interest charge for this).

What this example illustrates is that, when it comes to settling an inheritance tax bill, there's a big difference between cash and other fairly liquid assets held *inside* a pension and cash and other liquid assets held *outside* a pension.

Those held outside a pension can be used to settle an inheritance tax bill on illiquid assets like property without incurring additional income tax charges.

How Much Inheritance Tax?

In the examples that follow we take a look at *how much* inheritance tax could be payable on pension savings from 6th April 2027. Note there could be further changes before the draft legislation is finally passed. After this we will take a look at the *income tax* treatment of withdrawals from inherited pensions.

In all the examples below we assume the individual has a defined contribution pension plan (for example a SIPP). Defined benefit schemes are not covered in this guide.

To keep the examples simple we ignore the residence nil rate band for now. This provides an additional exemption of £175,000 (and sometimes £350,000 for a surviving spouse) for private residences left to direct descendants, typically children or grandchildren.

Example

June, a divorcee, dies aged 70 with a pension fund worth £300,000 and other investments worth £700,000. Her estate will be valued at £1 million for inheritance tax purposes and the inheritance tax bill is likely to be £270,000:

£1 million less £325,000 = £675,000 x 40% = £270,000

This equates to an overall tax rate for the estate of 27%. The inheritance tax on the pension pot will be £81,000 (£300,000 x 27%). If the pension administrator is directed to pay the tax bill, this will leave £219,000 in the pension for June's beneficiaries.

Example

Glynn, a widower, dies aged 80 with a pension fund worth £800,000 and other assets worth £825,000. The total value of his estate for inheritance tax purposes is £1,625,000. Glynn's wife left all her assets to him when she died so his estate would potentially have a nil rate band of £650,000. The inheritance tax payable would be £390,000:

£1,625,000 less £650,000 = £975,000 x 40% = £390,000

This equates to an overall tax rate for the estate of 24%. The inheritance tax bill on the pension pot will be £192,000 (£800,000 x 24%). If the pension administrator is directed to pay the bill, this will leave £608,000 in the pension for Glynn's beneficiaries.

Example

Bill dies aged 90 with a pension fund worth £400,000 and other assets worth £1 million. He leaves all of his assets to his wife and thus no inheritance tax is payable on either his pension fund or his other assets.

If instead he leaves his pension fund to his children, his £325,000 nil rate band may be available to reduce the inheritance tax payable on the fund. The amount of inheritance tax payable would then be £30,000:

£400,000 less £325,000 = £75,000 x 40% = £30,000

If the pension administrator is directed to pay the tax bill, this will leave a pension pot of £370,000 for Bill's children.

Residence Nil Rate Band

The £175,000 or £350,000 residence nil rate band cannot be allocated to your pension fund but it may reduce the amount of your other assets subject to inheritance tax, leaving more of the £325,000 or £650,000 nil rate band allocated to your pension.

This is how we would currently expect this to work:

Example
Heather, a widow, dies aged 85 with a pension fund worth £500,000 and other assets worth £900,000, made up almost entirely of her home. The total value of her estate for inheritance tax purposes is £1.4 million. Heather's husband left all his assets to her when he died and, as a result, her estate has a nil rate band of £650,000 and a residence nil rate band of £350,000.

The £350,000 residence nil rate band reduces the taxable value of her other assets from £900,000 to £550,000 and her overall taxable estate from £1.4 million to £1.05 million. Her £650,000 nil rate band may be allocated as follows between her pension and other assets:

Pension: £650,000 x £500,000/£1.05 million = £309,524
Other assets: £650,000 x £550,000/£1.05 million = £340,476

Inheritance tax of £76,190 may be payable on her pension (£500,000 – £309,524 = £190,476 x 40%). Inheritance tax of £83,810 may be payable on her other assets (£550,000 – £340,476 = £209,524 x 40%).

Loss of Residence Nil Rate Band

One harmful side effect of including pensions in individuals' estates for inheritance tax purposes is that some people will have their residence nil rate band reduced or taken away altogether.

Once your estate is larger than £2 million, the residence nil rate band is reduced. For every £2 your estate exceeds £2 million, £1 of your residence nil rate band is taken away.

The residence nil rate band is £175,000 but can be up to £350,000 on the death of the second spouse. Thus if a surviving spouse dies with an estate worth £2.7 million or more the residence nil rate band will be lost altogether.

Take the example of a surviving spouse who dies with a pension pot worth £700,000 and other assets of £2 million. Assuming the surviving spouse has both their own and their deceased spouse's nil rate band, the inheritance tax calculation on the death of the second spouse could look like this:

	Currently	**From 6th April 2027**
Estate (excl. pension)	£2,000,000	£2,000,000
Pension	Excluded	£700,000
Total estate	£2,000,000	£2,700,000
Nil rate band	£650,000	£650,000
Residence NRB	£350,000	£0
Taxable estate	£1,000,000	£2,050,000
Inheritance tax @40%	**£400,000**	**£820,000**

As we can see, including the £700,000 pension pot in the estate leads to a complete loss of the residence nil rate band and the tax bill increases by £420,000. Not only is inheritance payable on the pension, it is also payable on an additional £350,000 of the family home.

Income Tax on Inherited Pensions

The above examples show the amount of *inheritance tax* that may be payable on pension savings from 6th April 2027.

Once this tax has been paid any amounts paid out of the remaining pension fund to your beneficiaries may also be subject to *income tax* in their hands.

Note, in this section we are not talking about pension withdrawals that will qualify for the special income tax exemption covered earlier in this chapter. This exemption will be available when the pension's inheritance tax is not paid directly from the pension and is designed to prevent double taxation. We will assume all inheritance tax issues have been settled (for example, the inheritance tax has already been paid directly from the pension by the pension administrator).

Some commentators have pointed out that imposing inheritance tax and then income tax on inherited pensions will lead to a combined inheritance tax and income tax rate of up to 67%. The calculation of this combined tax rate can be illustrated with a simple example:

Pension savings on death	£1,000
Inheritance tax @ 40%	£400
Left for beneficiaries	£600
Income tax @ 45%	£270

The total tax payable is £670 which is 67%.

However, this simplistic bit of number crunching does not tell the whole story. The initial pension contributions will have enjoyed income tax relief, which means there is likely to be significantly more money saved up via a pension compared with alternative savings products.

For example, as we shall see in Chapter 16, someone who inherits a pension pot (and the tax-free lump sum that came out of it) could end up with between 16.67% and 41.67% more money than someone who inherits an ISA, despite the double tax charge on the inherited pension pot.

It's important to make this point so that people are not put off making pension contributions. Inheritance tax will not make pensions less attractive than other savings products from a tax saving standpoint. Although it will no longer be possible to use pensions as an "unlimited inheritance tax shelter", other products and assets like ISAs and buy-to-let property are, of course, already subject to inheritance tax.

Returning to income tax on inherited pensions, whether income tax will be payable by your beneficiaries depends on your age when you die. As a general rule of thumb:

- 75 or older – income tax payable by your beneficiaries
- Under 75 – no income tax payable by your beneficiaries

If you die before age 75 it is possible that income tax will be payable on part of any *lump sum* paid to your beneficiaries. But as we shall see, this income tax charge can be avoided in many cases.

Death at Age 75 or Older

After any inheritance tax has been paid (from 6th April 2027), your beneficiaries can inherit your remaining pension savings. They will also have to pay income tax on any money they withdraw.

Note, pension savings left to your spouse are exempt from inheritance tax but not income tax.

The funds can be paid out as an immediate lump sum or, if the pension scheme offers this facility, placed into beneficiary drawdown accounts.

With drawdown your beneficiaries will be able to keep the money invested and growing tax free for as long as they like, perhaps until they themselves retire. They can withdraw as much money as they like, whenever they like.

Taking an immediate lump sum or making a large withdrawal from beneficiary drawdown may result in a large income tax bill.

Example

Helen dies aged 80, leaving pension savings of £200,000 after her inheritance tax liability has been settled. Her son Glenn is the beneficiary. He earns a salary of £60,000 per year.

Helen's remaining pension savings are placed into a drawdown plan for Glenn and he withdraws £100,000 as income during a single tax year.

For the purposes of illustration, we'll assume future income tax rates and thresholds are the same as now. Glenn will end up paying additional income tax of £46,771 on the £100,000 pension withdrawal.

This is because, with total income of £160,000, he loses his personal allowance and pays 45% tax on a significant portion of the pension withdrawal.

It may be more tax efficient for Glenn to leave as much money as possible growing tax free in the drawdown plan until he himself retires and then start making gradual withdrawals, which may be taxed at just the 20% basic rate of income tax.

Death before Age 75

If you die before reaching age 75 your remaining pension savings (after any inheritance tax has been paid from 6th April 2027) can be paid out as a lump sum to your beneficiaries.

Alternatively, if the pension scheme allows it, your remaining pension pot can be converted into beneficiary drawdown accounts.

In most cases no income tax will be payable by your beneficiaries on either a lump sum payment or withdrawals from a beneficiary drawdown account.

However, with lump sums there is a cap on the amount of cash your beneficiaries can receive free from income tax.

Income Tax Treatment - Lump Sums

As mentioned in Chapter 3, the lifetime allowance has been scrapped and replaced by two new allowances:

- The Lump Sum Allowance – £268,275
- The Lump Sum and Death Benefit Allowance – £1,073,100

Both allowances limit the lump sums that can be paid out of your pension savings free from income tax. The Lump Sum Allowance was covered in Chapter 3 and is simply the amount of tax-free cash you can take when you start accessing your pension savings.

The Lump Sum and Death Benefit Allowance potentially limits the amount of any *lump sum* your beneficiaries can receive free from income tax, if you die before reaching age 75.

The standard lump sum and death benefit allowance is £1,073,100. It could be higher if you have lifetime allowance protection (something we don't cover in this guide).

Lump sum payments to beneficiaries that are within the available Lump Sum and Death Benefit Allowance are free from income tax where the pension scheme member dies before the age of 75, as long as they're made within two years of the pension scheme becoming aware of the death (otherwise they're taxable).

Amounts in excess of the deceased's Lump Sum and Death Benefit Allowance are subject to income tax in the hands of the beneficiaries.

Most tax-free lump sums paid during an individual's lifetime are deducted from the Lump Sum and Death Benefit Allowance, although there are some exceptions. Thus the allowance is typically reduced by any tax-free cash you've taken out of your pension and any tax-free serious ill-health lump sum you've received.

For example, someone who has taken £268,275 of tax-free cash out of their pension (the maximum for most people) will typically see their Lump Sum and Death Benefit Allowance reduced to:

£1,073,100 less £268,275 = £804,825

If that person dies before age 75 the first £804,825 of any *lump sum* payments made to beneficiaries will be tax free. Any excess will be subject to income tax in their hands.

Lump sums paid to beneficiaries out of pension savings that were crystallised (accessed) before 6th April 2024 are ignored because these pension savings will have already been tested against the old lifetime allowance. In other words, it should be possible to have them paid out free from income tax.

There's a lot more technical detail about the Lump Sum and Death Benefit Allowance that I'm not going to cover in this guide. For example, the amount deducted from £1,073,100 is calculated slightly differently for pension savings accessed before 6th April 2024 and this may affect the size of the allowance (see Chapter 3).

The reason I'm not going to cover the Lump Sum and Death Benefit Allowance in any more detail is because it's largely irrelevant if your pension savings can be placed into drawdown for your beneficiaries, instead of paid out as a lump sum.

Income Tax Treatment – Beneficiary Drawdown

Instead of taking a lump sum your beneficiaries can opt to have your remaining pension savings (after any inheritance tax has been paid from 6th April 2027) converted into beneficiary drawdown accounts.

This allows them to avoid the adverse income tax consequences that arise when the Lump Sum and Death Benefit Allowance is exceeded on a death before the age of 75.

The money will continue to grow tax free in the drawdown accounts and your beneficiaries can withdraw as much as they like free from income tax, whenever they like.

With beneficiary drawdown there is no cap on the amount of these tax-free withdrawals, even if the entire drawdown fund is paid out in one go. The Lump Sum and Death Benefit Allowance does not apply to beneficiary drawdown. It only applies to pension savings that are paid out as a lump sum to a beneficiary, without being placed into a drawdown account first.

The benefit of tax-free growth in beneficiary drawdown accounts should not be underestimated. It probably makes sense in many cases to not make large withdrawals if the money will end up in a taxed account subject to income tax and/or capital gains tax.

Your beneficiaries will have to request to have the inherited pension pot converted into beneficiary drawdown accounts. This will only be possible if the pension arrangement offers this facility (most modern defined contribution pension plans do but it's probably worth checking).

Finally note that where untapped pension savings are placed into drawdown for a beneficiary, withdrawals will only be tax free if the drawdown designation is made within two years of the pension scheme administrator becoming aware of the member's death.

Non-Resident Beneficiaries

We've discussed the benefits of beneficiary drawdown accounts several times in this chapter. Please note that most schemes will not permit a non-UK resident beneficiary to open a beneficiary drawdown account. In such cases the only alternative may be a lump sum payment. This may be something to bear in mind when deciding who should inherit your pension savings.

The Importance of Nominating Beneficiaries

It's important to let your pension provider know who you would like to inherit your pension pot.

You can nominate beneficiaries by completing a simple 'expression of wish' form. Many pension providers let you do this online nowadays.

You can pick as many people as you like, with a different percentage going to each, and update the form at any time.

Although these nominations aren't generally legally binding at present, they let the pension provider know your wishes, and are rarely ignored.

If you would like your *adult children* to inherit your pension savings, it's particularly important that the correct nominations are in place. This is so that they can enjoy all the benefits of beneficiary drawdown we've discussed in this chapter, rather than have the money paid out as a lump sum, which could be heavily taxed in their hands.

If your beneficiaries are not dependants and you have other dependants, your beneficiaries will only be able to choose drawdown if you have nominated them. If a non-dependant beneficiary has not been nominated, the only option will be a lump sum if there are any surviving dependants or someone else who has been nominated.

Dependants include your spouse or civil partner and children under the age of 23. Older children are also counted as dependants if they're dependent on you because of mental of physical impairment. An unmarried partner may also be classed as a dependant if they're financially dependent on you.

Thus in many cases your adult children will not be classed as dependants and will have to be nominated to ensure that they can benefit from beneficiary drawdown.

Note, the current practice of making nominations that are not legally binding may change after 5th April 2027, since the current benefit of keeping pension savings outside the estate for inheritance tax purposes will no longer apply.

Tax Planning

Make Bigger Pension Withdrawals?

Before it was announced that pensions would be subject to inheritance tax, financial advisers were advising wealthier retirees to spend their other savings and assets and keep as much money as possible in their pension pots to pass on free from inheritance tax to their children.

Should wealthier retirees now start withdrawing more money from their pensions to gift to family members?

It's impossible to provide a one size fits all answer because there are so many factors to consider. However, let's take a look at a simple example, focusing solely on the pension pot and ignoring other assets that could be gifted instead.

We'll assume inheritance tax is payable at 40% on any money remaining in the pension on death. Although the overall effective tax rate is likely to be less than 40%, thanks to the £325,000 nil-rate band and other exemptions, it is the 40% marginal tax rate that is more relevant when it comes to making tax planning decisions. As a simple example, someone with £2 million of assets who gives a child a £100 gift will reduce their estate by £100, potentially saving £40 inheritance tax, i.e. 40%.

We'll also assume the maximum 25% tax-free lump sum has already been taken from the pension because I suspect most people do this, often as soon as possible. (If a lump sum isn't needed it can always be gifted to family members and will typically fall out of the inheritance tax net after seven years.)

Example

Yvonne has a drawdown pension fund worth £100,000. She decides to withdraw all the money and give it to her son Michael. We'll assume she has other sources of income and therefore pays 40% income tax on all of the money she withdraws, leaving £60,000 to give to Michael. Providing she survives at least seven years there will be no inheritance tax payable on the gift.

(Note, Yvonne may have to make the pension withdrawals over several tax years to prevent her taxable income exceeding £100,000 which would see her income tax personal allowance withdrawn and her marginal income tax rate rise from 40% to 60%.)

Alternatively she could leave the £100,000 in her pension until she dies. After paying 40% inheritance tax this will leave £60,000 which can be placed into a beneficiary drawdown account for Michael. The money will continue to grow tax free but Michael will pay income tax on any money he withdraws (assuming Yvonne is 75 or older when she dies). Even if he only pays income tax at 20% on these withdrawals, he will be left with just £48,000, compared with the £60,000 he would end up with from a lifetime gift.

Even though Yvonne pays 40% income tax on all the money she withdraws from her pension during her lifetime and gives to Michael, this still leaves him better off than the alternative: inheriting a pension pot subject to inheritance tax and income tax in his hands.

And if Michael were to end up paying 40% income tax on his withdrawals from the inherited pension pot he would end up with just £36,000.

The best case scenario would be where Yvonne can arrange her affairs so that she only pays income tax at the 20% basic rate on some or all of the money she withdraws from her pension and gifts to Michael. If she can do this a total of up to £80,000 could be gifted to Michael over a number of years.

Michael could use the cash gifts to fund additional pension contributions of his own, attracting full income tax relief. Or he could perhaps invest the money gradually in an ISA where it will continue to grow tax free.

This example seems to show that lifetime pension withdrawals beat inherited pension pots. Does this mean Yvonne should withdraw as much money as possible from her pension and give it to Michael? Not necessarily because there could be other assets she may prefer to gift instead, with a lower overall income tax and inheritance tax bill.

Example continued
Let's say Yvonne also has an ISA worth £100,000. The following example compares a lifetime gift of pension savings with a lifetime gift of ISA savings. In both cases, we will assume Yvonne survives seven years after making her gifts so they escape inheritance tax.

Pension savings gifted, ISA left until death:
If Yvonne withdraws her pension savings during her lifetime and gives the money to Michael he will receive £60,000 (assuming Yvonne pays 40% income tax). If she leaves her £100,000 ISA intact, Michael will receive £60,000, after 40% inheritance tax has been paid. In total Michael will end up with £120,000.

ISA savings gifted, Pension left until death:
If she gifts Michael her ISA savings during her lifetime he will receive the full £100,000. When Yvonne dies Michael will inherit her pension pot: £60,000 after paying 40% inheritance tax. Michael will end up with £36,000 if he pays 40% income tax on his pension withdrawals. In total Michael will end up with £136,000.

In this example Michael ends up with more money if Yvonne leaves her pension savings intact and subject to inheritance tax and gifts Michael her ISA savings instead. This is because, with an inherited pension pot, Michael's taxed pension withdrawals will be smaller than Yvonne's taxed lifetime withdrawals. Michael will pay income tax on withdrawals of £60,000, whereas Yvonne would pay income tax on withdrawals of £100,000.

The extent of the savings and the overall outcome depends to a large extent on income tax rates: whether Yvonne will pay 20% or 40% income tax when she withdraws money from her pension to give to Michael and whether Michael will pay 20% or 40% on his own withdrawals if he inherits the pension pot instead.

Michael will end up even better off with an inherited pension pot (with £148,000 in total) if he can arrange his affairs so that he pays just 20% income tax on his withdrawals from the inherited pension as a basic-rate taxpayer.

Getting Yvonne to make pension withdrawals to gift to Michael would only make sense if she can pay just 20% income tax on her withdrawals **and** if he is likely to pay 40% income tax if he inherits her pension savings instead. The potential savings are fairly modest, however, and Michael could end up just £4,000 better off in this example.

Another point to consider is that an inherited pension pot might end up free of income tax if the original scheme member sadly dies before the age of 75: another reason why a lifetime gift of other assets might be preferable.

Assuming she does live to at least 75 though, the best outcome would be achieved if Yvonne gave Michael both her pension and ISA savings during her lifetime. Inheritance tax could be avoided altogether on both assets if she survives at least seven years. Of course most retirees cannot afford such generosity.

Pensions Left to Spouses

In the above example we assumed that the pension savings were left to a child. Many individuals will, of course, prefer to leave their pension savings to a surviving spouse. So the above example may only be relevant when there is no surviving spouse.

Income tax will still be payable on any withdrawals a surviving spouse makes from an inherited pension pot (for deaths after reaching age 75). However, there will be no inheritance tax payable at this point.

In light of the announcement that inheritance tax will be levied on pensions, some individuals who previously intended to leave their pension pots to their children, may now decide to change their nominations and leave them to their spouses instead.

And because the spouse exemption only applies to married couples, some unmarried couples with large pension pots may even decide to tie the knot!

Minimising Income Tax on Beneficiary Withdrawals

Parents who wish to pass on their pension pots to their children or other family may need to teach them how to withdraw the money tax efficiently. The savings will be maximised if your beneficiaries' withdrawals are taxed at the 20% basic rate of income tax or less.

This isn't a problem if you die before age 75 because your beneficiaries should be able to withdraw all the remaining money free from income tax (after any inheritance tax bill has been paid).

In this case it may be more tax efficient for them to withdraw all the money tax free rather than pass on the inherited pension pot to their own children (your grandchildren), who will probably have to pay income tax on their own withdrawals (if your children die after reaching age 75).

Your beneficiaries could also withdraw money from the inherited pension pot to fund pension contributions of their own. With higher-rate tax relief this could leave them significantly better off overall.

If you die after reaching age 75 the withdrawals made by your beneficiaries will be subject to income tax in their hands. In many cases your beneficiaries will still be working when they inherit your pension savings and could therefore end up paying income tax at 40%, 45% or even 60% on their withdrawals.

It may therefore be far less wasteful if they wait until they themselves retire before withdrawing money (when they will possibly be paying income tax at 20%). Such long-term planning can only be undertaken if the inherited pension pot is placed into beneficiary drawdown, rather than paid out as a lump sum.

Having said this, your beneficiaries could make tax-free withdrawals if they have no other income and the withdrawals are covered by their income tax personal allowance (currently £12,570). This may be the case if they are at university, starting a business or taking time off work to raise children.

Pension withdrawals taxed at 20% can be made by your beneficiaries as long as these withdrawals do not take them over the higher-rate threshold, currently £50,270. (For beneficiaries living in Scotland, the higher-rate threshold is currently £43,662 and income below this threshold is taxed at between 19% and 21% after deducting the personal allowance.)

In some cases leaving your pension savings to a less heavily taxed beneficiary may be worth considering. For example, it may be more tax efficient to leave them to a beneficiary who has no other taxable income or is a basic-rate taxpayer, rather than one who is a high income earner and pays income tax at 45%.

Next Time Around

Another reason it may make sense for your beneficiaries to withdraw as much as they can after they inherit your pension pot when it is either free from income tax or suffers income tax at no more than 20% is because, if they still hold that pension pot when *they* die, it could potentially suffer inheritance tax *again*.

For example, withdrawals that are either tax free or taxed at no more than 20% can be gifted by your children to your grandchildren and escape inheritance tax if your children survive seven years.

Alternatively, if your children are already well provided for, it may make sense to bypass the whole process and leave your pension pot to your grandchildren.

Tax-Free Lump Sums

Before the recent inheritance tax announcement some wealthy pension savers may have considered leaving ALL their pension savings intact for their beneficiaries, not even withdrawing their 25% tax-free lump sum of up to £268,275.

This may have been worth considering before age 75 when all your pension savings could potentially be left to your children free from both inheritance tax and income tax.

Once you reach age 75 your beneficiaries will pay income tax on all the money they withdraw, including what would have been your tax-free lump sum.

This strategy of not withdrawing tax-free cash before age 75 will become far less attractive once pensions become subject to inheritance tax from 6th April 2027.

It may be better to withdraw your full entitlement to tax-free cash and gift it to your children to save on inheritance tax.

Taxcafe's guide *How to Save Inheritance Tax* has a detailed chapter on IHT planning with pensions.

Chapter 11

How to Save Income Tax When You Tap Your Pension

When the pension withdrawal rules were relaxed back in 2015 there were fears that retirees would blow their pensions on expensive holidays and Lamborghinis. A few reckless individuals will no doubt squander their savings but the vast majority will probably withdraw the money gradually and spend it wisely.

Nevertheless, there is still a danger that even careful retirees will spend their savings a bit too quickly and end up depleting their pension pots.

Those who want a guaranteed income for life, with no danger of running out of money, can always hand over their retirement savings to an annuity provider. For example, a 65 year old with a £100,000 pension pot can currently buy a guaranteed income for life of around £5,145 per year. This will increase by 3% per year and continue providing a pension for their widow.

This is significantly higher than in recent years because annuity rates have risen in line with interest rates.

It may be possible to achieve a higher income by using a drawdown arrangement and investing in, for example, stock market companies with a long track record of paying growing dividends, or other investments. However, your income will not be guaranteed and could fall, as could the value of your investments.

This is the dilemma retirees face in the wake of the 2015 "pension freedoms" revolution. Freedom to spend your pension savings as you like does not necessarily make life any easier!

You should probably only spend a tiny fraction of your pension savings each year if they are to last through your retirement. The money you leave in your pension pot will continue growing tax free and any surplus funds can be passed on to your family, even if some inheritance tax is eventually payable.

Some retirees may wish to make bigger than normal withdrawals occasionally, not to fritter away but for other reasons such as to:

- Invest in an ISA
- Buy rental property
- Reduce mortgages or other debts
- Start a business

Tax will be an extremely important factor when it comes to deciding how much to withdraw from your pension and when. In this chapter we're going to take a closer look at some of the strategies pension savers may be able to follow to pay less income tax and capital gains tax.

These days retirees have the freedom to control their tax bills to some extent by making bigger pension withdrawals in some tax years and smaller withdrawals in other years.

Saving Income Tax

Any money you withdraw from your pension, over and above your 25% tax-free lump sum, is subject to income tax. If you withdraw a lot in one go you could end up paying tax at 40%, 45% or perhaps even 60% (if your withdrawals take your income over £100,000 and your personal allowance is withdrawn).

Most retirees should endeavour to pay no more than 20% basic-rate tax on their pension withdrawals. One way to achieve this is by spreading withdrawals over many tax years.

During the current 2026/27 tax year (and through to the end of the 2030/31 tax year) you will pay no more than basic-rate tax if your taxable income from all sources is less than £50,270. At present most retirees do not earn more than £50,270 per year and should therefore refrain from making big pension withdrawals that push them into the 40% tax bracket.

In Scotland the higher-rate threshold is currently £43,662. At this income level the tax rate increases from 21% to 42%.

Example

It's the start of the 2026/27 tax year. Andrew is 60 and earns a salary of £60,000. He has been saving into a pension and ISA. His pension pot is worth £200,000 and his ISA savings are worth £100,000. His wife Elizabeth is the same age and has similar income and savings.

If for whatever reason Andrew decided to withdraw all of his pension savings in one go, one quarter (£50,000) would be tax free. The remaining £150,000 would be fully taxed. His total taxable income would be £210,000 (£60,000 salary plus £150,000 of pension income).

With this much income, all of his pension income would be taxed at either 40% or 45% and he would lose his income tax personal allowance.

Andrew's total income tax bill would rise from £11,432 (salary only) to £80,703. He would end up paying tax at an effective rate of 46% on his pension withdrawal.

Furthermore, the money he takes out would no longer grow tax free outside his pension plan.

Fortunately, Andrew has no need to tap his pension pot at this time and realizes he is better off leaving the money alone while he is working full time.

He doesn't even want to withdraw his tax-free lump sum because he has no use for it at present and wants it to continue growing tax free.

In fact, instead of taking money out, he intends to keep putting money into both his pension and ISA. He enjoys higher-rate tax relief on his pension contributions.

This is one of the reasons why pension savers need to be careful about tapping their savings too early. If you are using flexi-access drawdown and withdraw any income over and above your tax-free lump sum, your future pension contributions could be limited to £10,000 per year (see Chapter 8).

A similar restriction applies if you withdraw any money as an uncrystallised funds pension lump sum (UFPLS).

Example continued

Three years later it's 2029/30 and Andrew is 63. He decides to resign from his job because he wants to work part time. His pension pot is now worth £280,000 and his ISA savings are worth £160,000. Before getting a part-time job he decides to take a year off to pursue various interests, including buying and renovating a rental property. Andrew and Elizabeth withdraw their 25% tax-free lump sums to purchase the property outright without a mortgage (£140,000 in total) and transfer the rest of their pension savings into drawdown plans.

Although the property will eventually produce taxable income and capital gains (whereas the money was growing tax free inside their pensions), Andrew and Elizabeth believe they have found a genuine bargain which makes up for the loss of tax relief.

Because he has no other taxable income in 2029/30, Andrew withdraws an additional £12,570 tax free from his pension to avoid wasting his income tax personal allowance. He could also withdraw some money taxed at just 20% (currently up to £37,700).

Because he has withdrawn income from his pension, his future pension contributions will be limited to £10,000 per year. This does not cause Andrew any concern.

Example continued

A year later Andrew is 64 and gets a part-time job earning £15,000. He also earns £5,000 rent from his share of the property. If he doesn't need more income he can leave his drawdown pot growing tax free. If he wants more income he will be able to withdraw around £30,000 taxed at just 20% (assuming the higher-rate threshold is still £50,270 in 2030/31).

Three years later Andrew is 67 and has reached state pension age and decides to stop working. His drawdown pot is now worth around £260,000 and his ISA savings have grown to £205,000. Coupled with Elizabeth's savings and the income from the rental property, he feels financially secure enough to retire.

His state pension and rental income use up his income tax personal allowance so he will pay at least 20% tax on any income he withdraws from his pension in future. Keeping an eye on how his drawdown investments are performing, he varies the amount he withdraws each year but makes sure he never pays 40% income tax.

Reducing Capital Gains Tax

Because retirees can choose how much money they withdraw from their pension pots each year, they can halt or reduce withdrawals in years they sell assets like rental property and reduce their capital gains tax bills.

This is because you only pay 18% capital gains tax (as opposed to 24%) to the extent your basic-rate band is not used up by your income. For example, at present if you don't have any taxable income you can have £37,700 of capital gains taxed at 18%.

The potential tax saving is £4,524 per couple:

£37,700 x 2 x 6% = £4,524

Example continued
Andrew and Elizabeth decide to sell their rental property because they don't want the hassle of managing tenants etc.

After deducting various buying and selling costs and their £3,000 annual CGT exemptions they expect to be left with taxable capital gains of £35,000 each. These amounts will be taxed at just 18%, providing they haven't withdrawn too much income from their pensions.

In the tax year before the sale takes place they therefore decide to make larger than normal pension withdrawals, making sure they stay below the higher-rate threshold to avoid paying 40% tax.

In the tax year in which the property is sold they reduce their pension withdrawals so that all of their capital gains are taxed at 18%. They live off the extra income they withdrew during the previous tax year.

Once the sale has taken place and they know how much, if any, of their basic-rate bands are left, they can withdraw some additional money from their pensions taxed at just 20%.

Leaving Pension Wealth to Your Family

When you die your remaining pension savings can be left to your family (e.g. your spouse, partner or children). No inheritance tax will be payable if the money is left to your spouse but it may be payable if left to anyone else. This is rare at present but will become the norm from 6th April 2027 (see Chapter 10).

After any inheritance tax has been paid, the money left inside the pension will keep growing tax free and your beneficiaries can make withdrawals as and when they like. Their withdrawals will be subject to income tax if you die after reaching age 75.

ISA savings can also be left to family members. These have always been subject to inheritance tax, unless left to your spouse. And only your spouse can transfer the whole amount into their own ISA so the money continues to grow tax free (see Chapter 16).

Example continued
When Andrew dies at age 85 his remaining pension savings are left to Elizabeth who has them transferred into a beneficiary drawdown plan (see Chapter 10). She also inherits his remaining ISA savings and is allowed to transfer them into her own ISA.

Elizabeth now has two drawdown plans. The investment growth in both is tax free but withdrawals from either plan will be subject to income tax. When she dies the remaining funds can be passed to her children, after any inheritance tax has been paid. The remaining funds can be transferred into beneficiary drawdown accounts where they will continue to grow tax free. Any withdrawals her children make will be subject to income tax (assuming Elizabeth dies after reaching age 75).

Her combined ISA savings also enjoy tax-free growth and all withdrawals will be tax free. When she dies the remaining funds can be passed to her children but cannot be left inside the ISA tax wrapper and will also be subject to inheritance tax.

If Andrew left all of his assets to Elizabeth, it's possible she will be able to leave up to £650,000 to her children free from inheritance tax (ignoring the residence nil rate band applying to the family home).

If she wishes to gift money to her children during her lifetime she may wish to choose between gifting her pension or ISA savings (see Chapter 10 for a full discussion).

Withdrawing Lump Sums Gradually

Retirees who wish to make occasional large lump sum withdrawals should try to spread them over several tax years wherever possible.

Example
Barbara normally has income of £40,000, made up of rental income, her state pension and withdrawals from her personal pension. During the current tax year she wants to withdraw an additional £20,000 to pay for a log cabin garden office. If she withdraws all of the money during the current tax year, almost £10,000 will be taxed at 40%. If she withdraws the money over two tax years she will pay tax at 20%. Her total tax saving will be almost £2,000.

Big Contributions Close to Retirement

Because retirees can make unlimited pension withdrawals, it may be worth making bigger than normal pension contributions when you are close to retirement.

Example
Alan and Betty are both 60 and each earn £65,000 per year. At present, they make gross pension contributions of around £5,000 per year each. Betty's mother recently passed away, leaving her £70,000. Betty decides to give half the money to Alan so they can both ramp up their pension contributions before they stop working in five years' time. The reason Betty gives half the money to Alan and the couple spread their increased contributions over five tax years is so that higher-rate tax relief can be enjoyed on all of the additional contributions (see Chapter 4).

They're happy to make these increased pension contributions in the knowledge that the money will not be locked up because they have both reached the minimum pension age (although there are drawbacks to withdrawing pension income early – see Chapter 8).

They personally invest £35,000 each over a five year period, making sure they always enjoy full higher-rate tax relief on their additional contributions (see Chapter 4). For example, in 2026/27 they can make an additional gross pension contribution of up to £9,730 each:

£65,000 income - £50,270 higher-rate threshold - £5,000 existing contribution

This means a cash pension contribution of up to £7,784 (£9,730 x 0.8).

Over the five year period they invest £35,000 each and the taxman will add £8,750 basic-rate tax relief to each pension pot, so they end up with additional pension savings of £43,750 each. They also enjoy additional tax refunds of £8,750 each (their higher-rate tax relief).

Ignoring any tax-free investment growth they enjoy on these additional pension contributions, when they retire they'll each be able to withdraw an additional tax-free lump sum of £10,938 (£43,750 x 25%).

The remaining money (£32,812 each) will be fully taxed when withdrawn. If we assume the withdrawals are taxed at just 20%, Alan and Betty will each be left with £26,250. Depending on how much other income the couple have, these taxed withdrawals may have to be made over several tax years to avoid paying tax at 40%.

In total the couple receive higher-rate tax relief of £17,500, tax-free lump sums totalling £21,876 and after-tax income totalling £52,500. So their £70,000 investment has been transformed into £91,876.

The reason Alan and Betty did so well is they spread their pension contributions over more than one tax year to maximize higher-rate tax relief and spread their withdrawals over more than one tax year to minimise their income tax bills.

It may also be worth making bigger pension contributions close to retirement even if you only enjoy basic-rate tax relief... but the benefits are far smaller.

Example
Emily is 60 and intends to retire next year. In recent years she has been investing just enough in her pension to maximise her higher-rate tax relief (see Chapter 4). She has £24,000 of surplus savings and decides to invest all of it in her pension. The taxman adds £6,000 of basic-rate tax relief so she ends up with additional pension savings of £30,000. There is no higher-rate tax relief on this additional contribution.

Soon after retiring she decides to withdraw the whole £30,000. One quarter (£7,500) will be tax free. Emily pays basic-rate tax at 20% on the remaining £22,500, leaving her £18,000. In total, Emily is left with £25,500, compared with her original investment of £24,000. She enjoys a £1,500 windfall from this simple piece of tax planning.

What the above examples reveal is that, where possible, pension contributions should always be spread over several tax years if this means more higher-rate tax relief can be enjoyed.

Big pension contributions that only result in basic-rate tax relief may still be worthwhile in some cases but the benefits are modest.

You also have to watch out for HMRC's recycling rules. These are designed to stop you taking a tax-free lump sum and reinvesting it in your pension with a second round of tax relief (see Chapter 9).

The recycling rules can also be triggered if you make big pension contributions in the two tax years *before* you start withdrawing money.

HMRC says that very few lump sums will be affected and the recycling rules are only triggered if you always intended your tax-free lump sum to be an integral part of paying for your increased contributions (either directly or indirectly).

Paying 40% Tax when You Retire

With the higher-rate threshold frozen at £50,270 for 10 years until 5th April 2031, there's a good chance some retirees, who expected to remain as basic-rate taxpayers, will start paying 40% instead of 20% income tax on some of their pension income in the years ahead.

This is even more likely to happen if you receive a second or third source of taxable income, for example your state pension or income from an inheritance.

Retirees who are currently basic-rate taxpayers but expect to become higher-rate taxpayers in the future, may wish to consider making bigger pension withdrawals taxed at just 20% now instead of at 40% in the future.

Those who have placed their pension savings into a flexible drawdown account can withdraw as much or as little income as they like each tax year and can therefore do this type of tax planning.

Example
Simon is 63 and has taxable income of £40,000 this year (2026/27) made up entirely of withdrawals from a pension drawdown account. He is a basic-rate taxpayer because his income is less than £50,270.

If he increases his pension withdrawals by 3.5% per year (to keep pace with inflation) his income will be around £46,000 in 2030/31, which will still be below the £50,270 frozen higher-rate threshold.

However, Simon will also turn 67 in 2030/31 and start receiving his state pension, which we will assume has grown to £14,400 by then.

Thus in 2030/31 Simon could have total taxable income of £60,400 (£46,000 + £14,400), with £10,130 of that taxed at 40% (£60,400 - £50,270).

Simon may therefore wish to consider reducing his private pension withdrawals in 2030/31, so that none of his income is taxed at 40%.

If he reduces his withdrawals by £10,130 to £35,870 then, along with his £14,400 state pension, his total taxable income will be exactly equal to the £50,270 higher-rate threshold.

In the next 2031/32 tax year (and future tax years) he should be able to increase his pension withdrawals to keep pace with inflation if, as expected, the higher-rate threshold is also increased with inflation.

Furthermore, to avoid wasting his basic-rate band over the next few years, Simon could consider making additional pension withdrawals taxed at just 20% until he reaches state pension age.

For example, this year Simon has taxable income of £40,000. This means he has £10,270 of his basic-rate band remaining (£50,270 - £40,000) and can make an additional pension withdrawal of £10,270 taxed at just 20%.

The after-tax amounts could be invested in an ISA so the money continues growing tax free.

Example

Ann is 75 and widowed and has income of £30,000 from her state pension and some rental properties. She also has a personal pension pot worth £200,000 from which she withdraws roughly £10,000 per year. Her total income is £40,000 so she only pays 20% tax.

Her mother Betty is 95 and lives in a nursing home. Ann expects to inherit all of Betty's assets when she dies, giving her additional taxable income of roughly £25,000 per year. With this extra income Ann will become a higher-rate taxpayer and will effectively pay 40% tax on any income she withdraws from her pension.

Before Betty dies Ann decides to withdraw an additional £10,000 per year from her pension and invest the money in an ISA where it will continue to grow tax free. She reasons that it is better to pay an additional £2,000 per year income tax now rather than £4,000 per year at some point in the future as a higher-rate taxpayer.

If Ann is worried about her eventual inheritance tax bill she could consider gifting the additional money she withdraws from her pension to her children or grandchildren, rather than invest it in an ISA.

They could use the money to fund pension contributions of their own or invest it in an ISA where it will continue growing tax free.

She could also consider halting all withdrawals from her pension after she inherits her mother's assets. This will allow her to avoid paying income tax at 40% on her withdrawals.

Her remaining pension pot may eventually be subject to inheritance tax but she may prefer to leave it intact and gift other assets to her children (see Chapter 10).

Retirees with significant assets face a difficult juggling act, deciding how much income to withdraw from their pensions and whether to gift any surplus pension savings or other assets to their children, taking account of both income tax and inheritance tax.

Summary

- It is possible to make unlimited pension withdrawals when you reach pension age (55 rising to 57 in 2028).
- Any money you withdraw over and above your tax-free lump sum will be subject to income tax.
- Many retirees can pay no more than 20% income tax and should avoid making withdrawals taxed at 40% or even 45%, where possible.
- This can be achieved by spreading withdrawals over many tax years, while keeping an eye on the £50,270 higher-rate threshold (£43,662 in Scotland).
- However, the freezing of the higher-rate threshold means some retirees could end up paying 40% instead of 20% income tax on some of their pension income in the years ahead.
- Taxable lump sum withdrawals should be spread over more than one tax year where practical.
- In most cases it will not be tax efficient to withdraw income if you are still working and a higher-rate taxpayer.

- In some cases it may be worth postponing pension withdrawals so that capital gains are taxed at 18% instead of 24%.

- Money left inside your pension pot when you die will be subject to inheritance tax from 6th April 2027, unless you leave the money to your spouse.

- Your remaining pension savings can be left to anyone, for example your children or grandchildren. After any inheritance tax has been paid (under current proposals) the remaining money will continue to grow tax free but income tax will be paid on any withdrawals they make (unless you die before age 75).

Chapter 12

Pensions versus Buy-to-Let

Should you withdraw money from your pension to buy property?

This would only be worth considering if you think you can earn a better *after-tax* return from property than from your *tax-free* pension investments (typically shares and bonds).

Investing in property has become less attractive following three tax changes in recent years:

- Additional stamp duty land tax (5% from 31st Oct 2024)
- Restricted tax relief on mortgage interest
- A 2% increase in income tax rates (from 6th April 2027)

Prior to April 2016 you wouldn't have paid any SDLT if you bought a rental property for £100,000... now you'll pay £5,000. You would have paid just £2,500 if you bought a property for £250,000... now you'll pay £15,000! (Different rates apply in Scotland and Wales.)

When you add legal fees and mortgage arrangement fees, buying investment property is much more expensive than buying stock market investments. With shares the stamp duty is typically just 0.5% and brokers' commission is usually just a few pounds.

Borrowing to buy property has also become much more expensive. Higher-rate tax relief for mortgage interest has been taken away and instead landlords receive a "tax reduction" equal to just 20% of their finance costs (22% from 6th April 2027).

The tax relief restriction only affects *residential* property businesses and does not apply to properties held inside companies.

The restriction to tax relief on interest costs is even more painful than the stamp duty increase because those affected feel its impact every year, not just when a new property is purchased.

See the Taxcafe guide *How to Save Property Tax* for more information.

Let's take a look at an example where the individual ends up better off by tapping their pension savings to invest in property (although some of the assumptions are, arguably, questionable):

Example
Hannah is 55, a higher-rate taxpayer and has a pension pot worth £90,000. She decides to withdraw all the money to pay the deposits on two buy-to-let properties which she thinks will perform better than her pension investments over the next 10 years.

The first 25% she withdraws is tax free and the rest is taxed at 40%, leaving her with a grand total of £63,000. Note, she will have to withdraw the money over more than one tax year to avoid going over the £100,000 threshold, which would result in a significant additional tax charge from the loss of her personal allowance.

(Withdrawing taxable income from her pension so many years before she retires is extremely aggressive. It means her future pension contributions will be limited to £10,000 per year – see Chapter 8.)

Using buy-to-let mortgages she acquires two properties for £100,000 each, with a £25,000 deposit and £75,000 mortgage on each property. The final £13,000 of her pension savings is used to cover her purchase costs (including stamp duty land tax of £10,000 and legal fees).

To make the example simple we'll assume she breaks even on the rental income side. All of Hannah's rental income goes towards paying mortgage interest, income tax and other costs associated with the property. Note, now that interest rates are significantly higher than in recent years it's possible she will incur an overall rental loss, which means she will have to find money from other sources to cover her costs.

We'll assume Hannah's properties grow by roughly 7% per year. 10 years' later, when she's 65, they're worth £400,000 in total. She decides to sell one property to pay off both mortgages and use the second property for retirement income. On the £200,000 property she sells she faces a capital gains tax bill and other selling costs of roughly £25,000. After paying off both mortgages (£150,000 in total) she's left with £25,000 in the bank and a fully paid up property worth £200,000.

How would she have fared by keeping her pension investments instead? If we assume they also would have grown by roughly 7% per year, after 10 years she'd end up with around £180,000. She could withdraw 25% tax free and, assuming the rest was withdrawn gradually and taxed at just 20%, she would end up with £153,000 in total.

In summary, with a pension she ends up with £153,000, with property she ends up with £225,000 – almost 50% better off.

Hannah does much better with property despite paying 40% tax on all the money she takes out of her pension to fund the purchases and despite having to pay capital gains tax when she sells one of the properties.

Of course, the only reason the properties did better is because they were heavily geared up with borrowed money and then rose in value. This is an extremely high-risk strategy and probably only suitable for experienced property investors who are many years away from retirement (i.e. closer to 55 than 65).

Geared investments almost always do better than ungeared investments when things go to plan and the assets rise in value. If the properties had fallen in value significantly, Hannah could have lost all of her capital.

Borrowing heavily to invest in property worked best when interest rates were very low. Now that interest rates are significantly higher, coupled with the fact that tax relief on mortgage interest is restricted, it is much harder to make an overall rental profit on a heavily geared property investment.

In some cases property investors with big mortgages like Hannah will be making rental losses, which means they will require money from other sources to subsidize their property investments.

What about using your pension savings to invest in property without a mortgage? Let's take a look at a simple example:

Example
Bill is 60 and retired and has a pension pot worth £150,000 (he has already taken his tax-free lump sum), as well as other taxable income of roughly £20,000 per year.

He currently withdraws the income generated by his pension investments but wants to keep the capital intact for his children. His pension savings are invested in funds earning 4% income per year: £6,000 or £4,800 after 20% income tax has been paid when withdrawn from his pension.

He wants to know if he could get more income by withdrawing all his pension savings to buy a rental property outright without a mortgage.

If he withdraws all his pension pot in one go he'll pay 40% income tax on most of the money. He will also lose his personal allowance and some of the money will be taxed at 45%. So we'll assume he withdraws £50,000 per year over three tax years, paying basic-rate tax on just over half his withdrawals and 40% tax on the rest, leaving him with roughly £108,000.

He then buys a rental property for £100,000, using the final £8,000 to cover his stamp duty and legal fees. If the £100,000 property is to generate more income than the £6,000 produced by his pension investments, it would need to have a rental yield significantly higher than 6%. This is because with property there are lots of additional costs (repairs, insurance, letting agent fees etc) and there are bound to be empty periods as well. It's also worth adding that, from 6th April 2027, the income tax rates on rental income will be 2% higher than those applying to pension income.

It is possible to find properties with higher rental yields (in some parts of the country they are higher, in others parts they are lower) but it's probably unlikely Bill will end up with *significantly* more income after deducting the various expenses he will incur.

The problem with using pension savings to buy an expensive asset like property outright is that it may be necessary to spread the pension withdrawals over many tax years to avoid paying income tax at 40% or more.

And what about Bill's children? When he dies they'll either inherit a pension pot worth £150,000 or a property worth £100,000, plus any capital growth on the investments. Both would potentially be subject to inheritance tax (pensions from 6th April 2027).

Bill's children will probably pay income tax on any money they withdraw from an inherited pension. If they pay just 20% income tax they could end up better off inheriting a pension. If they pay 40% or more they could end up better off inheriting a property.

In summary, it is possible to deplete your pension savings to invest in property. However, this strategy is only likely to leave you better off if you're prepared to accept much more risk (i.e. borrow money) or you expect property to deliver significantly higher returns than pension investments (typically shares and bonds).

Chapter 13

Drawdown vs Annuities

When you retire you may prefer to use your retirement savings to buy an annuity, rather than use flexi-access drawdown (see Chapter 8).

Annuities offer an important benefit: a guaranteed income for life. This may appeal to older retirees who don't want the hassle of managing investments and desire what is as close as it gets to a risk-free income.

Annuity rates were very low for many years but are much more attractive these days now that interest rates have risen significantly. The life insurance companies that offer annuities take your cash and invest it in long-term gilts (debt issued by the UK Government). When gilt yields increase, so too do annuity rates.

The table on this page on Hargreaves Lansdown's website shows you how much retirement income you could end up with, depending on your age and the type of annuity you buy:

www.hl.co.uk/retirement/annuities/best-buy-rates

For example, at the time of writing a 65 year old with £100,000 of pension savings could purchase an income of £5,365 per year and that income will increase in line with the retail prices index, to protect against inflation. A 75 year old could receive an income of £7,312 per year. These are amounts are subject to income tax.

One thing many people don't like about annuities is that when you die your annuity payments will generally stop. So if you die too soon you may not get your money's worth. This is because annuities are all about pooling risk – those that live longer than average are subsidized by those who live shorter than average.

Many people also fear that annuity providers skim off a big chunk of their money in charges.

There are solutions to both of these concerns. For example, you can buy an annuity that guarantees to keep paying out for a set number of years (even up to 30 years) whether or not you're still alive, or an annuity that keeps paying out to your spouse or partner.

You can also shop around for the best rate (the highest income) and there are many online resources to help you do this. There is often a significant difference between the best and worst deals on offer.

However, once you have purchased your annuity there is no going back. For example, you can't switch to another provider offering a better deal. Buying an annuity is a lifelong commitment.

It's important to stress that the choice between using flexi-access drawdown or buying an annuity doesn't have to be an all or nothing one. Some retirees may use some of their pension savings to purchase an annuity, so that they have some guaranteed income, and keep their remaining savings in drawdown to top up their income and cover one-off expenses.

Although annuities offer lots of benefits, there are several reasons why flexi-access drawdown may be more attractive than buying an annuity immediately when you retire:

Benefit #1 – Take the Tax-free Cash and Keep Working

When you reach age 55 (57 from 2028) you may want to get your hands on your 25% tax-free lump sum but keep working for another 10 years or even longer.

Any additional income you take from your pension pot while you are still working (for example annuity income) could be taxed at 40% or more if you also have income from a job or business.

Because there is no requirement to withdraw income from a flexi-access drawdown arrangement, you can postpone withdrawing income until you actually retire and your income tax rate falls.

While you are working your pension savings can continue to grow tax free.

Benefit #2 – Keep Your Favourite Investments

If you opt for an annuity you generally have to sell your pension investments and hand over your savings to an insurance company. This is not an attractive proposition if you are confident your pension investments will perform well.

With a drawdown pension you can enjoy the best of both worlds: an income and tax-free investment growth on the money left inside your pension plan.

Benefit #3 – Wait for Better Annuity Rates

Many pension experts argue that you should ultimately use your pension savings to buy an annuity because the income is more secure than drawdown income (the income never falls no matter how long you live and no matter what happens to interest rates and the value of investments).

The problem is that, although annuity rates are relatively attractive at present, this may not be the case when *you* retire, for example if interest rates fall significantly in the years ahead.

One solution is to start your retirement with a drawdown pension and make a phased exit, using some of your drawdown money to buy an annuity at regular intervals when annuity rates are attractive.

Benefit #4 – Wait until Age 75

If you die before reaching age 75 your remaining drawdown pension savings can be paid out to your beneficiaries (for example your children) free from income tax. But if you die after reaching age 75 your beneficiaries will pay income tax on any money they receive and they could end up paying up to 40%, 45% or even 60% tax, depending on how much other income they have.

Age 75 may therefore be considered a potential tipping point for buying an annuity.

Before reaching age 75 you may prefer to hold onto your pension savings so that your beneficiaries can inherit what's left in your drawdown fund free from income tax.

Once you reach age 75 your pension savings are arguably a bit less valuable to your beneficiaries, so you may prefer to use them to buy yourself a more secure annuity income. Your beneficiaries may not inherit anything (unless your annuity comes with some sort of guarantee) but you, at least, can eliminate the risk of outliving your assets.

Furthermore, annuity rates are significantly higher if you're 75 compared with, say, 65 (annuity rates increase with age).

Benefit #5 – Reduce Your Income and Save Tax

If you can vary your income from year to year, as you can with drawdown (but not with an annuity) you can do some constructive tax planning. This is very useful in years when your tax bill may spike because you receive big one-off receipts such as capital gains.

Let's say you sell an asset and the capital gain is £50,000. If you reduce your drawdown income in the same tax year, so that your basic-rate band is not fully utilised, you will pay 18% tax instead of 24% tax on some of your capital gain.

The basic-rate band is currently £37,700 so the maximum potential tax saving from paying 18% capital gains tax instead of 24% tax is currently:

£37,700 x 6% = £2,262

This tax saving could potentially be enjoyed every time you sell an asset subject to capital gains tax.

It is also possible to achieve further capital gains tax savings by spreading asset sales across several tax years because this lets you make use of more than one annual CGT exemption. Unfortunately this additional saving is smaller than in the past because the annual CGT exemption has been cut from £12,300 to £3,000. The additional annual saving from spreading sales across several tax years is now just £720 (£3,000 x 24%).

Annuities after Death

If you are receiving income from a standard "single life" annuity, no money will be payable to your family (for example your spouse or children) after you die.

However, there are lots of bells and whistles that can be added to ensure payments continue after your death. These usually come at a price – a lower starting income.

Joint-Life Annuities

If you have purchased a joint-life annuity the income payments will continue after your death, typically at a reduced rate such as 50%. The second person will typically be your spouse or unmarried partner but could be another family member.

Although pensions will become subject to inheritance tax from 6th April 2027, joint-life annuities will be exempt, even if the payments continue to someone other than your spouse. This is because their right to receive a continuing income is considered separate from your estate.

Guarantee Periods and Value Protection

Some annuities pay out for a guaranteed period after you die. For example, if you have a 10 year guarantee period and die after 3 years, your beneficiary will receive income payments for the remaining 7 years.

Another benefit you can add is 'value protection'. Your beneficiary will receive a lump sum if you die before the total income paid out equals the purchase price of the annuity. For example, if you pay £100,000 for an annuity and die after receiving payments of £30,000, your beneficiary will receive £70,000.

From 6th April 2027 payments under guarantee periods and value protection lump sums will be included in your estate for inheritance tax purposes. However, they will be exempt from inheritance tax if paid to your spouse.

Income Tax

If you die before age 75, payments made to your beneficiary under an annuity contract will generally be tax free. If you die when you are 75 or older, the payments will be subject to income tax in the hands of your beneficiary.

Part 3

Pensions vs ISAs

Chapter 14

Introduction

Which is better: an ISA or a pension?

This is an important question because ISAs and pensions are the two most popular savings vehicles for individuals.

Both offer tax-free growth (your investments will grow free from income tax and capital gains tax), making them far more attractive than taxed investment accounts in most cases.

However, when it comes to saving tax there are no ifs, buts or maybes: pensions are a **much** more powerful tax shelter for most higher-rate taxpayers.

With ISAs there is no up-front tax relief on the money you put in but withdrawals are tax free. With pensions there is up-front tax relief but most withdrawals are taxed. At first glance the two tax reliefs appear quite different but, as it happens, tax-free withdrawals (ISAs) and up-front tax relief (pensions) produce exactly the same result, even though the tax savings are enjoyed at different points in time.

However, there are two reasons why pensions are normally a much better income tax shelter, especially for higher-rate taxpayers:

- **Tax-free lump sum**. Not all of your pension withdrawals are taxed. You can take one quarter as a tax-free lump sum (up to £268,275).
- **Retirees usually pay less tax**. If your tax rate falls from 40% to 20% when you retire – as it will for most higher-rate taxpayers – a pension could save you a lot more tax than an ISA. This is because you will enjoy 40% tax relief on the money you put in but will pay no more than 20% tax on the money you take out.

Thanks to these two factors it is quite possible that a pension will generate 41.67% more after-tax income than an ISA, as we shall see in Chapter 15.

Other Tax Differences

Pensions and ISAs are treated differently in other respects which may be important in some circumstances:

Tax When You Emigrate

If you become non-UK resident your income and capital gains sheltered inside an ISA will continue to be tax free. Tax free in the UK that is. The amounts may be taxed in your new country of residence. For example, the Isle of Man Government specifically states in its tax return booklet that an ISA's tax-free status "does not apply in the Isle of Man and you should declare any income from these products".

The tax-exempt status of pensions, however, is recognized in most countries, although they are arguably less portable assets (you can withdraw all your ISA savings easily if you emigrate).

Withholding Taxes on Dividends

These days it is easy for stock market investors to buy shares in overseas companies, the most popular being US companies.

It's important to note that dividends from overseas companies are often subject to withholding tax.

In the US the dividend withholding tax rate is 30%. However, in terms of the double tax agreement between the US and UK, the amount of withholding tax can be reduced by completing an IRS form W-8BEN. Most investment platforms will handle these forms on your behalf so the process is relatively simple.

However, there is an important difference between US shares held in pensions and ISAs. The double tax agreement provides a specific exemption for pensions, which means US dividends paid to a pension scheme will not have any US withholding tax deducted.

The double tax agreement does not recognize ISAs. ISA investors are subject to the same reduced withholding tax rate as everyone else: 15%.

ISAs – Protection from Greedy Politicians

Although pensions are arguably a better tax shelter, one tax benefit unique to ISAs is protection from future income tax increases. Money withdrawn from ISAs is tax free, whether those withdrawals take place next year or in 30 years' time.

But if the Government decides to increase income tax rates, you could end up paying more than you expected on your pension income.

During your long and happy retirement there are likely to be many different governments, all with the power to dictate how much tax you pay on your pension withdrawals. And there's no denying that Britain has had its fair share of barmy taxes. In 1974 the top income tax rate on earnings was 83% and the top rate on investment income was 98%.

Do you believe that no politician will increase your income tax further at any time over the next 20 to 30 years? If you do think significant income tax increases are a possibility, it may be a good idea to put some of your retirement savings into an ISA.

ISAs are not, however, completely immune from politicians. There were rumours in the press in recent years about a lifetime cap being placed on ISA savings to limit the number of 'ISA millionaires'. Nothing has been announced to date.

Lifetime ISAs

Those aged 18 to 39 can open a Lifetime ISA which can be used to save for a first home or for retirement. In this guide we will focus on the second retirement option.

Any money you put in (up to £4,000 per year) receives a 25% Government bonus. So if you put in £4,000, the Government will add £1,000. This is the same as the basic-rate tax relief on pension contributions.

It's possible to continue making contributions up to age 50. This means you could potentially invest up to £128,000 between age 18 and 50 with a Government bonus of up to £32,000.

Contributions to a Lifetime ISA fall within the overall £20,000 ISA subscription limit. So if you invest £4,000 in a Lifetime ISA you can invest another £16,000 in other ISAs.

You can open more than one Lifetime ISA during your lifetime (as long you're under 40) but can only pay into one per tax year.

Lifetime ISAs – Early Withdrawals

Unlike a pension, your savings are not locked up inside a Lifetime ISA. However, if you withdraw money before reaching age 60, for any reason other than to buy your first home, there will normally be a 25% early withdrawal charge.

This will claw back all of the Government bonus, plus an additional 6.25% of the amount you invested.

For example, if you invest £1,000, the Government will add £250, giving you total savings of £1,250. If you then decide to withdraw the money, the 25% penalty will be £312.50, leaving you with £937.50. Thus you will lose the Government bonus plus an extra £62.50 (6.25%) out of the amount you originally invested.

This charge effectively also applies to any growth in the value of your savings.

Where an individual is diagnosed with terminal ill health, they can withdraw all their Lifetime ISA savings tax free (including the bonus), regardless of age.

Lifetime ISAs – Saving for Retirement

If you use your Lifetime ISA to save for retirement, funds can be withdrawn from age 60.

As we shall see in Chapter 15, a Lifetime ISA could be an attractive alternative to saving in a pension if you are a basic-rate taxpayer. Like pensions they attract a top up from the Government but, unlike pensions, ALL the money you take out will be tax free.

However, it would probably be unwise to stop making contributions to a workplace pension if that means forfeiting your employer's contribution (which is effectively 'free' money).

Lifetime ISAs – Big Changes Ahead

As announced in the November 2025 Budget, the Government is exploring replacing the Lifetime ISA with a new savings vehicle for first-time homebuyers.

The Government has also stated that: *"It will remain possible to open a lifetime ISA until the new product becomes available and for account holders to continue to save into their lifetime ISA in line with the existing rules indefinitely."*

Those under 40 who do not currently have a Lifetime ISA, but think they may benefit from using this product as a retirement savings vehicle, should consider opening one before it's too late.

You could pay in just the minimum amount required to open the account (which could be £100 to £250 depending on which investment platform you use) and make no further contributions until you are confident saving in a Lifetime ISA will be beneficial.

ISAs – Non-tax Benefits

- **Flexibility.** With an ISA you can access your savings *at any time.* You can also withdraw and replace cash from your ISA without it counting towards your annual ISA subscription limit, as long as the repayment is made in the same tax year as the withdrawal. (Note not all ISA providers offer this.) At present pension savers can only access their money when they reach age 55 (rising to age 57 in 2028 and probably higher at some point in the future). Having £100,000 sitting in your pension isn't much use if you need emergency cash.

- **No age limit**. In practice you cannot keep contributing to a pension indefinitely. Once you reach age 75 you will not receive tax relief on your contributions. There is no upper age limit for ISA investments and you can withdraw money and make new contributions continually.

- **No earnings required.** If you want to contribute more than £3,600 per year to a pension with tax relief you need 'earnings'. There is no such restriction on ISA investments, although the maximum annual investment is currently capped at £20,000.

Pensions – Non-tax Benefits

- **Investment limits.** The maximum annual investment is £60,000 and the carry-forward rules allow a contribution of up to £240,000. However, as we saw in Chapter 4, the maximum contribution you can make with higher-rate or additional-rate tax relief may be a lot lower than these limits.

- **Investment choice**. Pensions offer a slightly wider choice of investments than ISAs. For example, ISAs cannot be used to invest directly in commercial property whereas pensions can.

- **Protection from creditors**. In the event of bankruptcy, pension savings held inside an HMRC approved pension are generally protected from creditors (most occupational and personal pensions are HMRC approved). Money withdrawn from a pension can potentially be claimed for a period of time.

Chapter 15

Case Study: ISA vs Pension

In this chapter we'll follow two investors building up a retirement nest egg over 10 years and see who ends up better off:

- Peter – Pension investor
- Ian – ISA investor

Both are higher-rate taxpayers and invest £6,000 per year. Peter makes an initial contribution of £8,000 to which the taxman adds a further £2,000 of basic-rate tax relief.

He then claims back £2,000 when completing his tax return. All in all Peter has £10,000 of pension savings that have only cost him £6,000.

Ian also invests £6,000 per year out of his own pocket in an ISA. He doesn't enjoy any tax relief on his contributions so his total investment is just £6,000. Note Ian invests in a traditional ISA. We'll compare pensions and Lifetime ISAs shortly.

Both Peter and Ian enjoy investment returns of 7% per year. These returns are completely tax free for both the ISA investor and the pension investor.

We track how both investors perform from year to year in Table 2. At the end of year 1 they have £10,700 and £6,420 respectively, which is simply their initial investments of £10,000 and £6,000 plus 7% tax-free investment growth.

After five years Peter has £24,613 more than Ian and after 10 years he has £59,134 more than Ian. Even though they're both earning an identical tax-free return of 7% and investing the same amount of money out of their own pockets, Peter is much better off because his annual investment is boosted by income tax relief on his contributions.

In fact, Ian always has just 60% as much money as Peter. Peter's extra 40% is thanks to the income tax relief he receives on his pension contributions.

Table 2
Pension Savings vs ISA Savings

End Year	Pension £	ISA £
1	10,700	6,420
2	22,149	13,289
3	34,399	20,640
4	47,507	28,504
5	61,533	36,920
6	76,540	45,924
7	92,598	55,559
8	109,780	65,868
9	128,164	76,899
10	147,836	88,702

After-tax Comparison

Although Ian's retirement savings are much smaller than Peter's, that's not the whole story. Firstly, Ian enjoyed much more flexibility along the way and could have taken money out of his ISA at any time. Peter can only withdraw money from his pension when he's 55 or older.

Secondly, Ian can withdraw all his ISA savings *tax free*. Peter will have to pay income tax on any money he withdraws over and above his 25% tax-free lump sum.

If he withdraws all his pension savings in one go he'll pay income tax at 40% or more on a lot of the money. However, because these are *retirement savings* we will assume Peter only withdraws a little bit of money each year to avoid depleting his capital too quickly and pays income tax at the 20% basic rate.

But before we do this let's pretend Peter has to pay 40% tax on all his pension withdrawals and is not entitled to tax-free cash. How do ISAs and pensions compare then?

40% Tax, No Tax-Free Lump Sum

After paying 40% tax on all of his withdrawals Peter the pension saver would be left with £88,702:

£147,836 less 40% tax = £88,702

Ian the ISA investor is left in an identical position:

£88,702 less 0% tax = £88,702

Thus, if you enjoy 40% tax relief on your contributions but pay 40% tax on your withdrawals, an ISA and pension produce the same outcome.

This is an interesting result if you have already built up significant pension savings: enough to use up your £268,275 entitlement to tax-free cash and to push you into higher-rate tax in retirement.

If you are already making full use of your £20,000 ISA allowance, it may still be worth making additional pension contributions so that, as with an ISA, you benefit from tax-free growth.

40% Tax, Tax-Free Lump Sum

Peter in this example has not used up his £268,275 Lump Sum Allowance and can take a 25% tax-free lump sum of £36,959 (£147,836 x 25%). He'll only pay tax on the remaining £110,877.

If we assume he pays 40% tax on the rest of his pension withdrawals his position after tax is as follows:

Tax-free lump sum:	£36,959
After-tax income (£110,877 less 40% tax):	£66,526

Peter is left with a total of £103,485 compared with Ian the ISA investor's £88,702.

This means Peter has 16.67% more money than Ian.

So even if you pay 40% tax on your pension income when you retire you could still receive more after-tax income from a pension than an ISA, thanks to the tax-free lump sum.

You could end up paying tax at 40% on some or all of your pension withdrawals if you have income from other sources, for example from rental property.

You could also end up paying tax at 40% on some of your withdrawals if you have built up a large pension pot and therefore have a large pension income.

20% Tax and Tax-Free Lump Sum

Finally, we'll assume that Peter, like many other retirees, is a basic-rate taxpayer when he retires. Peter's after-tax position is now as follows:

Tax-free lump sum: £36,959
After-tax income (£110,877 less 20% tax): £88,702

Peter is left with a total of £125,661 compared with Ian the ISA investor's £88,702.

Peter the pension saver ends up with 41.67% more money than Ian the ISA investor.

This example shows that, if you are a higher-rate taxpayer while you are saving for retirement and a basic-rate taxpayer when you retire, you will end up significantly better off using a pension instead of an ISA to save for retirement.

Tax-Free Pension Withdrawals

In the above example Peter pays 20% income tax on all of his pension income. The implicit assumption is that his income tax personal allowance, currently £12,570, is used up by other taxable income, perhaps his state pension and income from rental properties or a part-time job or part-time business.

I taxed all of his private pension income at 20% because I did not want to overstate the benefits of pension saving. In reality, some of the income you receive from a private pension plan may be tax free thanks to your personal allowance.

Once you reach state pension age your state pension could use up most if not all of your personal allowance. However, you can start withdrawing income from your other pensions roughly 10 years earlier.

If during this period your taxable income from other sources (for example rental property) does not use up all of your personal allowance, some of your pension income will be tax free.

If some of your pension income will be tax free, this naturally makes pensions even more attractive than ISAs for retirement saving.

Basic-Rate Taxpayers

In the above example Ian and Peter were both higher-rate taxpayers when they were making contributions. How do pensions and ISAs compare if you're a basic-rate taxpayer (income under £50,270 at present) and only enjoy basic-rate tax relief?

Let's assume that Ian and Peter are basic-rate taxpayers. Ian has £1,000 to invest in an ISA, Peter has £1,000 to invest in a pension.

Peter makes a cash contribution of £1,000 and the taxman adds £250 of basic-rate relief, leaving him with total pension savings of £1,250. Ian invests £1,000 in an ISA but doesn't receive any tax relief on his contributions so his total savings come to £1,000.

Now as it happens we can completely ignore any further contributions they may decide to make and their investment returns. These do not alter the outcome in any way.

In the previous examples we compared the fortunes of Ian and Peter after they had made contributions for 10 years. However, the final outcome would have been exactly the same after one year, two years or any number of years.

Their investment returns are also irrelevant as long as we assume that they enjoy identical tax-free returns. This is a reasonable assumption to make because pension and ISA savings can be invested largely in the same types of asset (if anything pensions offer a bit more flexibility, for example by allowing you to invest in commercial property).

Basic-Rate Taxpayer in Retirement

If we assume that Peter the pension saver is also a basic-rate taxpayer when he retires his after-tax position will be as follows:

Tax-free lump sum: £312.50
After-tax income (£937.50 less 20% tax): £750

Peter is left with a total of £1,062.50 compared with Ian the ISA investor's £1,000.

Peter is just 6.25% better off than Ian.

If you ask me this is not sufficient reward for putting your money in a locked box until you are at least 55. It's one reason why some basic-rate taxpayers may consider postponing contributions until they become higher-rate taxpayers (see Chapter 18).

Investing in a pension will, however, be more appealing if Peter expects some of his taxable pension income to be covered by his personal allowance or, more importantly, if he belongs to a workplace pension scheme and his employer is making additional contributions.

Higher-Rate Taxpayer in Retirement

What if Peter is a basic-rate taxpayer when he is making pension contributions but ends up paying higher-rate tax on his pension income?

This could happen if, for example, he eventually inherits or accumulates a significant amount of other assets such as rental property.

His after-tax position will then be as follows:

Tax-free lump sum:	£312.50
After-tax income (£937.50 less 40% tax):	£562.50

Peter is left with a total of £875 compared with Ian the ISA investor's £1,000.

Peter is 12.5% worse off than Ian.

This is the worse possible outcome when it comes to saving in a pension. And I don't think it's a completely unrealistic outcome. There are surely some pension savers out there who are enjoying just basic-rate tax relief on their contributions but will ultimately pay 40% tax when they withdraw those same contributions.

Summary

Pensions are extremely valuable tax shelters *in the right circumstances.* They're most attractive when you enjoy higher-rate tax relief (40%) on your contributions but only pay basic-rate tax (20%) on your taxable withdrawals. In this case you could end up with 41.67% more income that someone who uses an ISA to save for retirement.

The various examples we have looked at are summarised in the table below. For example, someone who enjoys higher-rate tax relief on their contributions and also pays higher-rate tax on the taxable withdrawal could end up with 16.67% more income than someone who uses an ISA to save for retirement.

	Basic-rate tax	**Higher-rate tax**
Basic-rate relief	6.25%	-12.5%
Higher-rate relief	41.67%	16.67%

Remember too that pensions are also more attractive if you expect some of your taxable withdrawals to be covered by your personal allowance or if you also receive contributions from your employer.

Freezing the Higher-Rate Threshold

Throughout this guide I have stated that many retirees are basic-rate taxpayers. This is because most people see their income fall fairly significantly when they retire: usually to a level well below the current £50,270 higher-rate tax threshold.

While this will probably remain true for most individuals it's possible that many readers will end up as higher-rate taxpayers when they retire. This is because the higher-rate threshold has been frozen for a whopping 10 years until 5th April 2031. And this tax policy was introduced at a time of high inflation.

Thus in the future, some pension savers, who expected to pay no more than 20% tax on their pension withdrawals, will pay 40% tax on *some* of their withdrawals.

Those wealthier pension savers who already expected to pay 40% tax on some of their pension withdrawals will now pay 40% tax on *more* of their withdrawals.

Some individuals who are currently basic-rate taxpayers, receiving just basic-rate tax relief on their pension contributions, may end up paying higher-rate tax on some of their pension withdrawals.

The freezing of the higher-rate threshold will thus alter the relative attractiveness of pensions over other savings products.

Lifetime ISA vs Pension

Those aged 18 to 39 can currently open a Lifetime ISA which can be used to save for a first home or for retirement (see Chapter 14 for more on forthcoming changes).

It's possible to invest up to £4,000 per year with a 25% Government bonus and continue contributing up to age 50.

The Lifetime ISA is an attractive alternative to saving in a pension if you are a basic-rate taxpayer. Like pensions they attract a top up from the Government but, unlike pensions, ALL the money you take out will be tax free.

For example, if you are a basic-rate taxpayer and invest £1,000 in either a pension or a Lifetime ISA you will receive a £250 top up from the taxman, leaving you with £1,250 in either account.

When you retire, however, withdrawals from the Lifetime ISA will be tax free, whereas only 25% of the money withdrawn from the pension will be tax free. The rest will be subject to income tax (although some of your pension income may also be tax free thanks to your personal allowance).

Let's say you pay tax at the 20% basic rate on your pension income. If we ignore investment growth to keep the example simple (it doesn't affect the outcome), with a Lifetime ISA you will end up with £1,250, with a pension you will end up with just £1,063 after tax.

Thus, if you're a basic-rate taxpayer, your retirement income could be 17.6% higher with a Lifetime ISA.

Lifetime ISA vs Pension – Higher-rate Taxpayers

Higher-rate taxpayers will generally get more bang for their buck from a pension.

For example, if you invest £1,000 in a Lifetime ISA you will receive a £250 top up from the Government leaving you with £1,250.

Because higher-rate taxpayers also receive a tax refund when they contribute to a pension (higher-rate tax relief) they can make bigger initial contributions. For example, if you invest £1,333 in a pension (£1,000/0.75) you'll receive a £333 top up from the Government, leaving you with £1,666 in your pension.

You'll also receive higher-rate relief of £333 (£1,666 x 20%) so, as with a Lifetime ISA, the investment will only cost you £1,000 personally (£1,333 investment less £333 higher-rate relief).

Ignoring investment growth, when you retire your £1,666 pension pot will become £1,416 (after taking 25% tax free and assuming the rest is taxed at 20%), compared with the £1,250 you would receive from a Lifetime ISA.

Thus, your retirement income could be 13% higher with a pension.

But if you end up paying higher-rate tax on your pension income you will end up with only £1,166 from a pension, compared with £1,250 from a Lifetime ISA.

Thus your retirement income could be 7% higher with a Lifetime ISA.

There are other important differences between Lifetime ISAs and pensions. With pensions your money is locked up until you're 55 (rising to 57 in 2028 and possibly higher in future years). With Lifetime ISAs you'll lose the Government top up and normally pay a penalty if you withdraw anything before age 60, unless the money is used to buy your first home. The rest of your savings can be withdrawn at any time.

If the pension is a company scheme, the additional contribution from your employer will make investing in such a scheme more attractive than a Lifetime ISA in most circumstances. In other words, you should probably not opt out of your employer's pension scheme to invest in a Lifetime ISA.

Make Mine a Double!

It *may* be possible to invest in a Lifetime ISA and then, when you're 60, take the money out and stick it into a pension, thereby enjoying two rounds of tax relief.

For example, if you invest £1,000 in a Lifetime ISA you will receive a 25% Government bonus, leaving you with £1,250. Ignoring investment growth, when you're 60 you will be able to withdraw the £1,250 tax free and may be able to invest it in a pension.

Because higher-rate taxpayers also receive a tax refund when they contribute to a pension (higher-rate tax relief), they can make bigger initial contributions. So instead of investing just your Lifetime ISA savings of £1,250 in your pension, you may be able to invest £1,667 (£1,250/0.75).

You'll receive £417 of basic-rate tax relief from the taxman, leaving you with £2,084 in your pension. You will also receive higher-rate relief of £417 (£2,084 x 20%), so the investment will only cost you £1,250 personally (the amount withdrawn from the Lifetime ISA).

Ignoring investment growth, when you eventually retire your £2,084 pension pot will become £1,771 (after taking 25% tax free and the rest taxed at 20%), compared with the £1,250 you would receive from your Lifetime ISA alone.

Thus your retirement income could be 41.67% higher than someone who invests in a Lifetime ISA only.

And your retirement income will be 77% higher than someone who invests in a traditional ISA only (ignoring investment growth they would end up with just £1,000).

It's impossible to say whether anyone will be able to benefit from this potential "tax loophole".

Because only those who are under 40 can open a Lifetime ISA and because withdrawals are only possible from age 60, it will be a good few years before anyone can attempt this tax relief double. Tax and pension rules will no doubt change a lot between now and then and the future of the Lifetime ISA is currently somewhat in doubt.

Chapter 16

ISAs vs Pensions: Inheritance Tax Planning

Your Spouse

There is generally no inheritance tax on any asset left to your spouse.

Your spouse can usually inherit your ISA savings with no inheritance tax payable AND invest them in their own ISA so that any future income and capital gains will continue to be tax free.

This was not possible a few years ago – your spouse could inherit your ISA savings but they were taken out of the ISA wrapper. What happens now is your spouse will receive a special expanded ISA allowance when you die which will allow them to put all your ISA savings into their own ISA. The technical term for this special ISA allowance is the "additional permitted subscription".

This tax concession is available to married couples and civil partners but is not available to unmarried couples.

How do ISAs compare with pensions?

Your spouse can also usually be left your pension pot with no inheritance tax payable. The fund can be converted into a beneficiary drawdown plan, allowing your spouse to withdraw money as and when they like (see Chapter 10). The investments in the drawdown plan will continue to grow tax free.

If you die before age 75 your spouse will not have to pay income tax on any money withdrawn from the drawdown plan. If you die after reaching age 75, they will pay income tax on any withdrawals.

If your spouse already has significant pension savings or other taxable income of their own and inherits a second pension pot from you, it's possible that any additional withdrawals they make from the second pension pot will take them over the higher-rate threshold (currently £50,270) and be taxed at 40%.

For this reason it may be preferable, in some cases, for married couples to spend more of their pension savings, rather than their ISA savings, as long as no more than 20% income tax is paid on the additional pension withdrawals.

The surviving spouse can then inherit a larger quantity of ISA savings and make tax-free withdrawals from them.

Unmarried couples who inherit ISA savings cannot keep them inside the tax wrapper. This means they may pay tax on any *future* income and capital gains. However, the surviving partner can gradually reinvest the inherited money in their own ISA.

Your Children

If you leave your ISA or pension savings to your children, they will form part of your estate for inheritance tax purposes (generally only from 6th April 2027 in the case of your pension).

Inheritance tax at 40% is payable on assets that exceed the threshold – currently £325,000, but up to £650,000 for widows or widowers. An additional nil rate band of £175,000 is also available for the family home (up to £350,000 for widows or widowers).

Any ISA savings your children inherit will be stripped of the tax-free ISA wrapper.

If your children inherit your pension savings and the funds are placed into beneficiary drawdown accounts the money will continue to grow tax free and they can withdraw it as and when they like.

If you die before age 75 your children will not have to pay income tax on any money they withdraw from the beneficiary drawdown account. If you die after reaching age 75 they will pay income tax on any money they take out.

If your children are working when they inherit your pension savings, there's a good chance they will end up paying 40% or perhaps even 45% income tax on any money they withdraw, unless they leave the money untouched until they themselves retire (and hopefully only pay income tax at 20%).

Pension Contributions vs ISA Contributions

In Chapter 10 we noted that, if your children inherit your pension savings, there could be a double tax charge in the future: firstly inheritance tax and then the remaining money could be subject to income tax in their hands.

Does this make pension contributions less attractive than ISA contributions when it comes to leaving money to your children?

Most certainly not! Your initial pension contributions will have enjoyed income tax relief (possibly at 40% or more) which means there is likely to be significantly more money saved up in a pension compared with an ISA.

In Chapter 15 we showed that, if you enjoy 40% higher-rate tax relief when you make pension contributions and pay 20% income tax on the money you withdraw (after taking your tax-free lump sum), you could end up with 41.67% more money overall than someone who invests in an ISA.

Exactly the same relative outcome can be obtained if you leave the same money to your children.

Inheritance tax may be payable, reducing the amount of ISA or pension savings your children can inherit (as well as the tax-free lump sum you've taken from your pension) **BUT** if your children pay just 20% income tax on any money they withdraw from the inherited pension pot, they could end up with 41.67% more money compared with inheriting an equivalent amount invested by you in an ISA.

Even if they end up paying 40% income tax on their withdrawals from the inherited pension they could end up with 16.67% more money. (From Chapter 15 we know that this is also how much better off you will be if you pay 40% income tax on any pension withdrawals you make during your lifetime.)

In summary, even after pension savings left to anyone other than your spouse become subject to inheritance tax from 6th April 2027, it will probably still be worthwhile making pension contributions (compared with other investments), even if those contributions end up being left to your children.

Pension Contributions vs ISA Contributions: No Tax-Free Lump Sum

In Chapter 3 we discussed whether pension contributions are still worth making for retirement income purposes, if you expect your existing savings to already use up your £268,275 tax-free cash allowance. The conclusion was that, even without the benefit of tax-free cash, additional pension contributions may be worth making, as long as you expect to pay income tax at the same rate or at a lower rate in the future.

But what if the additional pension contributions you make are not extracted but remain in your pension pot until you die? Again exactly the same relative outcome is obtained if you leave the same money to your children.

Inheritance tax may be payable, reducing the amount of ISA or pension savings your children can inherit but if you enjoy 40% tax relief when you make the pension contributions and your children pay 20% income tax on the money withdrawn from the inherited pension pot, they will end up with 33% more money compared with inheriting an equivalent amount invested by you in an ISA.

If your children end up paying 40% income tax on the money they withdraw from the inherited pension pot, they will end up with exactly the same amount of money as an equivalent investment made by you in an ISA.

In summary, even if your existing pension savings are likely to use up your £268,275 tax-free cash allowance, additional pension contributions may be worth considering, especially if you are already making full use of your £20,000 ISA allowance.

A Final Note on ISAs

What attracts so many people to ISAs is their flexibility. You can withdraw money at any time. Pension investors have to wait until they reach the minimum retirement age of 55 or older. As with everything in life, a compromise is usually the best solution: saving with both a pension and ISA. And as we shall see in Part 4, an ISA may be a great place to park money **before** you invest it in a pension.

Chapter 17

Pensions vs Taxed Accounts

In Chapter 15 we compared pensions and ISAs and showed that you could end up with up to 41.67% more money with a pension, after all income tax has been paid.

In this chapter we will compare pensions with *taxed* savings and investment accounts.

This chapter is relevant to those who are already making full use of their £20,000 annual ISA allowance and have surplus funds sitting in a taxed savings account or share dealing account. Such individuals are subject to income tax on their interest or dividend income and capital gains tax on their capital gains.

There are several reasons why an increasing number of individuals will be fully utilising their annual ISA allowance, ending up with savings in taxed accounts, and why those taxed accounts have, in recent times, become even less attractive from a tax standpoint:

- **ISA Freeze** – The overall ISA allowance has been frozen at £20,000 since 2017/18 and will remain frozen until 5th April 2031. If it had increased with inflation, it would be around £30,000 today and perhaps around £35,000 by April 2031.

- **Cash ISA Cut** – The maximum amount you can subscribe to cash ISAs will be reduced from £20,000 to £12,000 from 6th April 2027. Those age 65 and over will be unaffected.

- **Personal Savings Allowance Freeze** – The personal savings allowance allows basic-rate taxpayers to receive £1,000 of tax-free interest and higher-rate taxpayers to receive £500 (additional-rate taxpayers cannot benefit). These amounts have never been increased since the allowance was introduced in April 2016 and should be around 50% higher today to compensate for inflation.

- **Interest Income Tax Increase** – From 6th April 2027 the income tax rates applying to interest income are increasing by 2%. Thus higher-rate taxpayers will pay 42% on interest income that exceeds their £500 personal savings allowance. Those with income between £100,000 and £125,140 will typically pay 62%.

- **Dividend Tax Increase** – From 6th April 2026 the income tax rates applying to dividend income have been increased by 2%. Higher-rate taxpayers will now pay 35.75% (except for the first £500 which is tax free). Those with income between £100,000 and £125,140 will typically pay 58.25%. Additional-rate taxpayers will continue to pay 39.35%.

- **Tax Threshold Freeze** – The freezing of the £50,270 higher-rate threshold and £100,000 threshold (where your personal allowance is withdrawn) means more and more taxpayers are likely to see their interest and dividend income taxed at higher rates.

- **Other Harmful Side Effects** – All interest and dividends earned outside an ISA count as taxable income for the purposes of the withdrawal of the personal allowance (income over £100,000), the child benefit charge, and certain other charges.

- **Capital Gains Tax Increase** – The CGT annual exemption used to be £12,300 but is now just £3,000. The capital gains tax rates applying to stock market investments were also increased in 2024. Higher-rate taxpayers now pay 24% (previously 20%).

If you have money sitting in a taxed account is it possibly a good idea to stick it in a pension?

You can probably guess the answer is yes for many people – if pensions are better than tax-free ISAs they must surely be better than taxed accounts. The question is how much better?

Let's take a look at a simple example. All the usual assumptions and caveats apply: for example the individual doesn't mind tying up more money in a pension, has sufficient taxable income to enjoy full higher-rate relief on the additional pension contributions and will be able to withdraw 25% tax free in the future (i.e. their current pension contributions will not use up their £268,275 Lump Sum Allowance).

We will also ignore things like the personal savings allowance and dividend allowance – we'll assume these allowances are already being fully utilized. We will also assume that all interest income is taxed at 42% (the new rate applying from 6th April 2027).

Example

Zara is a higher-rate taxpayer and has £10,000 of surplus savings sitting in a taxed investment account earning 5% interest per year. After paying 42% income tax her money grows by just 2.9% per year, which would leave her with £13,309 after 10 years.

Instead she decides to stick the whole £10,000 in her pension. She also invests an additional £3,333 she has access to. The taxman tops up her £13,333 contribution to £16,667. She receives £3,333 of higher-rate relief when she submits her tax return (£16,667 x 20%). In summary, she ends up with £16,667 sitting in her pension at a net cost of £10,000.

After 10 years growing at 5% per year tax free she will have £27,148 in her pension, compared with £13,309 in a taxed account.

When she withdraws the money from her pension, 25% will be tax free and the rest taxed at 20% (assuming she is a basic-rate taxpayer in retirement). Zara will be left with £23,076 after tax compared with £13,309 from a taxed investment account.

Zara ends up with 73% more money by investing her surplus savings in a pension.

This example contains quite a few assumptions. If we modify them the outcome will be different. For example:

- **Income tax rate on pension withdrawals.** We assume Zara will pay 20% income tax on her taxed pension withdrawals. If she pays 40% income tax she would still end up 43% better off with a pension compared with a taxed investment account.

- **Tax-free lump sum availability.** If we assume Zara's existing pension savings will already use up her £268,275 Lump Sum allowance, she will pay income tax on ALL of the additional pension savings when she withdraws them. Even if she pays 40% income tax on all of these withdrawals, she could still end up 22% better off than with a taxed investment account. This is because she will still enjoy tax-free growth in her pension whereas she would pay income tax each year on the interest earned in a taxed account.

It's important to point out that making a pension contribution in this "worst-case" scenario (tax-free growth but no tax-free lump sum and all withdrawals taxed at 40%) still produces an identical outcome to investing through an ISA. This is worth noting if you are making full use of your £20,000 annual ISA allowance and have surplus cash sitting in a taxed account.

- **Investment time horizon and growth rate**. In the example we assumed Zara earns 5% for 10 years. The outcome will be different if we change either of these assumptions. If she invests for longer and/or enjoys a higher return a pension will produce an even better outcome, and vice-versa.

Capital Gains Tax

In the above example we assumed Zara pays 42% income tax every year on her interest income in a taxed account. However, if she invests in something like an equity fund, most of the growth will come in the form of capital gains (although there will possibly be regular dividend income too).

Her capital gains will be taxed at no more than 24% in a taxed account and this will only be payable when the asset is sold, possibly many years in the future. This is better than paying 42% tax every year and reduces the relative attractiveness of shifting money from a taxed account to a pension.

Having said this, equities often produce significantly higher returns over time than interest-earning investments, so you could still end up significantly better off sheltering them in a pension instead of a taxed account.

For example, if we assume Zara's investments grow by 8% per year for 10 years she could end up 63% better off with her money in a pension instead of a taxed account.

(The assumptions here include: 40% tax relief on additional pension contributions, 25% withdrawn tax free after 10 years, remainder taxed at 20%, all returns outside a pension subject to CGT at 24% in year 10.)

If Zara pays 40% income tax on her taxed pension withdrawals, instead of 20%, she could end up 34% better off with her money in a pension instead of a taxed account.

And if her existing pension contributions will already use up her Lump Sum Allowance and all of her additional pension savings are taxed at

40% when withdrawn, she could still end up 15% better off in a pension compared with a taxed account.

As mentioned above, it's important to point out that making an additional pension contribution in this "worst-case" scenario – no tax-free lump sum and all withdrawals taxed at 40% – still produces an identical outcome to investing through an ISA.

Additional Contributions Less Attractive

In all of the above examples we assumed Zara enjoys full higher-rate tax relief on her additional pension contribution.

This is only possible if she has sufficient taxable income above the £50,270 higher-rate threshold. For example if she has earnings of £80,000 and is already making gross pension contributions of £10,000, she can make an additional gross contribution of up to £19,730 with full higher-rate relief (£80,000 - £10,000 - £19,730 = £50,270).

But if she has earnings of £65,000 she can only make an additional contribution of up to £4,730 with full higher-rate relief (£65,000 - £10,000 - £4,730 = £50,270). Any further contribution will only enjoy 20% basic-rate tax relief.

Making additional pension contributions that only enjoy basic-rate tax relief will be much less attractive if she expects to ultimately pay 40% income tax when she withdraws the money.

Summary

The above examples show that if you are already making pension contributions and full use of your £20,000 annual ISA allowance, it may be worth considering further pension contributions if you have additional funds in some kind of taxed account.

How much better off you could be will depend on how well your investments perform over time and your personal circumstances: how much tax you are paying in the taxed account, how much tax relief you will enjoy on the additional pension contributions and how much tax you will pay when you withdraw the additional pension savings.

It's important to remember that money in most savings accounts and share dealing accounts can be accessed at short notice, whereas money in a pension is locked up until you are age 55 (57 from April 2028).

Part 4

Postponing & Accelerating Pension Saving

Chapter 18

Basic-Rate Taxpayers: Should They Make Pension Contributions?

Financial advisors usually advise people to start making pension contributions as early as possible. They often point to the 'magic' of compound interest. Compound interest – earning interest on interest – seems to possess magical powers, making millionaires out of just about anyone who starts early enough.

However, it's important to not confuse saving in a pension with saving *generally*. It's never too early to start saving... but it may be too early to start saving in a pension.

In previous chapters I have shown that higher-rate taxpayers enjoy twice as much tax relief on their pension contributions as basic-rate taxpayers. A higher-rate taxpayer is currently someone who has taxable income of more than £50,270 (£43,662 in Scotland).

So the question is: should you delay making pension contributions if you are currently a basic-rate taxpayer but expect to become a higher-rate taxpayer in the future?

More specifically, should you invest your savings somewhere else, for example in an ISA, and transfer the money into a pension when you will enjoy much more income tax relief?

This is the question we will answer in this chapter.

Are You a Temporary Basic-Rate Taxpayer?

There are lots of reasons why an individual may be a basic-rate taxpayer in one tax year but a higher-rate taxpayer in another. The most obvious reason is career progression: a graduate earns a lot less income than someone with the same qualifications and 20 years' experience. You may start your working life as a basic-rate taxpayer and become a higher-rate taxpayer a few years later.

Many self-employed business owners who are normally higher-rate taxpayers may become basic-rate taxpayers from time to time, for example if their income falls during an economic downturn or if they have higher than normal tax-deductible expenditure, for example if they make significant investments in equipment during the tax year.

Many company directors are also basic-rate taxpayers in some years but higher-rate taxpayers in other years, for example if they pay themselves a small dividend during one tax year and a big dividend during another tax year.

Finally, with the higher-rate threshold having been frozen at £50,270 for 10 years (from 6th April 2021 to 5th April 2031), many people are becoming higher-rate taxpayers simply because their pay has increased with inflation. (Similarly, many existing higher-rate taxpayers are seeing more of their income taxed at 40%, allowing them to make bigger pension contributions with 40% tax relief.)

Wealth Warning

There is one group of individuals who should always consider making pension contributions, even if they are only temporary basic-rate taxpayers: company employees who belong to workplace pension schemes. For them tax relief is only one of the benefits of making pension contributions. The employer will often match, or more than match, the contribution made by the employee – effectively handing over free cash which no sensible person would turn down (more on this in Chapter 23).

Case Study – Postponing Pension Contributions

Penny and Isabella are both basic-rate taxpayers but expect to be higher-rate taxpayers in three years' time. Both want to save £3,000 per year but they have different strategies. Penny decides to put her savings in a pension straight away because her father has advised her to start saving for retirement as soon as possible. Isabella also wants to save for her retirement but she also wants to maximise her tax relief. She decides to invest in an ISA until she is a higher-rate taxpayer and then transfer the money into a pension.

Who ends up better off?

Table 3
Pension vs ISA
Temporary Basic-Rate Taxpayers

End Year	Pension £	ISA £
1	4,013	3,210
2	8,306	6,645
3	12,900	10,320

We'll assume they both enjoy investment returns of 7% per year (tax-free inside both an ISA and pension). Penny's £3,000 annual investment is topped up with £750 of free cash from the taxman so her gross pension contribution is £3,750. After a year this will have grown to £4,013. After three years she will have £12,900.

Isabella's £3,000 ISA investment will be worth £3,210 after one year. After three years she will have £10,320. The results are summarised in Table 3. For every £1 Penny has in her pension, Isabella has just 80p – the difference is down to the 20% basic-rate tax relief Penny enjoys on her pension contributions.

Becoming Higher-rate Taxpayers

It's the start of the fourth tax year and Isabella knows her income will be well over the higher-rate threshold this year. So she decides to take her £10,320 ISA savings and stick them into her pension plan. The taxman will add £2,580 in basic-rate tax relief and, hey presto, she has £12,900 sitting in her pension plan, just like Penny.

However, as a higher-rate taxpayer, Isabella can also benefit from higher-rate tax relief. To calculate this we simply multiply her gross pension contribution by 20%:

£12,900 x 20% = £2,580

In summary, Penny and Isabella have both saved exactly the same amount of money but, because Isabella waited until she had enough income taxed at 40% before making pension contributions, she ends up with £2,580 more than Penny.

Maximising the Pension Pot

In the above example Isabella has the same amount of money as Penny in her pension plus a tax refund from HMRC. However, if Isabella would prefer to maximise her pension savings she could do things slightly differently.

What she could do is make a bigger pension contribution – £13,760 instead of just her £10,320 ISA savings. The taxman will top this up with £3,440 to produce a gross pension contribution of £17,200.

Isabella won't be out of pocket despite making a bigger contribution because she will also receive a tax refund of £3,440 (£17,200 x 20%) – her higher-rate relief.

This means the amount she personally contributes will simply be the amount she has saved up in her ISA:

£13,760 pension contribution *minus* £3,440 tax refund = £10,320

Now look at the size of Isabella's pension pot. She has £17,200 compared with Penny's £12,900 – 33% more money!

33% – The Magic Number

The same 33% increase in pension savings can potentially be enjoyed by anyone who postpones making pension contributions while temporarily a basic-rate taxpayer.

Regardless of whether you postpone for one year, 10 years or any other time period, and regardless of whether you are making big or small pension contributions, the result is exactly the same:

Your pension pot will be 33% bigger

Finally, remember that, although Isabella postpones her pension contributions, she does NOT postpone saving. Note too that she invests in an ISA so that, like Penny, she does not miss out on tax-free growth.

Practical Pointers

- The assumption is that Isabella enjoys the maximum higher-rate tax relief on her £17,200 pension contribution. However, we know from Chapter 4 that Isabella will only enjoy full higher-rate tax relief if she also has at least £17,200 of income taxed at 40%. If she doesn't, she will have to spread her pension contributions over more than one tax year.

- Isabella personally contributes £13,760, which is more than her £10,320 ISA savings. However, when she gets her tax refund back she is not left out of pocket. How do we calculate the number £13,760? Simply divide £10,320 by 0.75.

Chapter 19

Higher-Rate Taxpayers: Can They Put Off Pension Saving?

In the previous chapter it was shown that basic-rate taxpayers may be better off, in some circumstances, postponing pension contributions until they become higher-rate taxpayers.

What about higher-rate taxpayers – can they also put off making pension contributions?

While financial advisors usually tell people to start making pension contributions as soon as possible, it's important to not confuse the benefits of saving in a pension with the benefits of saving *generally*.

There are lots of reasons why you might not feel like putting much money into a pension right now, even though you would receive lots of tax relief. It all revolves around the potentially lengthy jail sentence placed on pension savings – you can't access them until you are 55 or older.

If you have big financial commitments, for example a mortgage or children's education to pay for many years, you may be very reluctant to tie up too much of your savings in a pension.

You certainly should be wary of making significant pension contributions if you are in imminent danger of losing a big chunk or all of your income, for example if your business is struggling or you are about to lose your job.

Am I saying it's not necessary to save in these situations? No, I'm a big fan of saving from day one. What I am saying is that you don't necessarily have to save a lot via a pension... not at certain stages of your life at least. It's a fat lot of good having £100,000 in your pension pot if your home is about to be repossessed.
Before making significant pension contributions, you should always make sure you have sufficient money saved elsewhere to protect against:

- An unforeseen drop in income, and
- Unforeseen expenses

But what about all the tax savings enjoyed by pension savers? If you delay putting money into a pension, won't you lose out? This is one of the great misconceptions about pensions.

As it happens, if you want immediate access to your savings, you don't have to put money into a pension until you are ready.

You will not be one penny worse off than someone who makes pension contributions continually for many years.

I've never heard any pension experts make this crucial point. Maybe it's because advising people to put off making pension contributions is bad for business, a bit like a tobacco company telling you to quit smoking.

Case Study – Postponing Pension Contributions

In Chapter 15 we compared Peter the pension saver with Ian the ISA investor. What we discovered is that pensions are much more powerful than traditional ISAs – you could end up with up to 41.67% more retirement income from a pension.

However, it is possible that Ian, the ISA investor, will have the last laugh. Let's say he originally started saving into an ISA because he wanted access to his savings. Back then he was worried about losing his income and also had a big mortgage and three children to support. Move forward five years, he's no longer worried about his income, the mortgage is smaller and the children have all flown the nest.

So he decides to take his ISA savings and stick them into a pension. Will he end up worse off than Peter, who started saving in a pension five years earlier?

Peter and Ian's savings up to the end of year five are summarised in Table 4. Just to recap, both are higher-rate taxpayers and both personally invest £6,000 per year. Peter enjoys income tax relief so his gross pension contribution is £10,000 per year, compared with Ian's £6,000 ISA investment. They both enjoy tax-free growth of 7% per year. After one year their £10,000 and £6,000 initial investments will be worth £10,700 and £6,420 respectively (explaining the first numbers you see in the table).

Table 4
Postponing Pension Contributions
Higher-Rate Taxpayers

End Year	Pension £	ISA £
1	10,700	6,420
2	22,149	13,289
3	34,399	20,640
4	47,507	28,504
5	61,533	36,920

After five years Peter has £61,533, compared with Ian's £36,920. Ian now takes his ISA savings and sticks them in a pension. Because he knows he'll get a tax refund (his higher-rate tax relief) he actually makes an investment of £49,226 (£36,920/0.75). The taxman adds £12,307 of basic-rate tax relief and, hey presto, Ian ends up with £61,533 sitting in his pension pot – exactly the same as Peter!

Ian also gets a tax refund of £12,307 (£61,533 x 20%), so his £49,226 pension investment costs him just £36,920 personally – exactly the amount he accumulated in ISAs.

In summary, Peter started saving in a pension from day one, whereas Ian put his savings into an ISA, before transferring the money into a pension five years later. By postponing his pension contributions, Ian was able to access his savings in the event of a financial emergency. Postponing his contributions has not left him out of pocket.

Postponing Pension Contributions – The Dangers

I'm not encouraging anyone to postpone making pension contributions. The point of this exercise is to show that, all things being equal, there is *mathematically* no difference between regular pension contributions and a big catch-up pension contribution. Saving in a pension over many years will not leave you better off.

As with everything, compromise is often the best solution. There's nothing to stop you making some pension contributions now and further catch-up contributions when your personal financial situation is healthier.

There are also some dangers and some very important practical issues when it comes to postponing pension contributions:

Danger # 1 Higher Rate Tax Relief Could Be Scrapped

We discussed this danger in Chapter 6. For many years there have been fears that higher-rate tax relief on pension contributions will be scrapped.

Many higher-rate taxpayers may therefore feel that it is wise to not postpone making pension contributions and make hay while the sun is still shining, i.e. make pension contributions NOW while higher-rate tax relief is still available.

Danger # 2 Loss of Employer Pension Contributions

If you belong to a workplace pension scheme to which your employer is contributing, postponing your own contributions could prove costly: you will lose the free cash being offered by your employer (see Chapter 23).

Danger # 3 Your Earnings Fall

If your income falls and you are no longer a higher-rate taxpayer when the time comes to make catch-up contributions, you will not enjoy any higher-rate tax relief.

This could happen if you own a business that enters a long tough patch or period of decline. It could also happen to a company employee who suffers redundancy and is unable to find another job that pays as well.

Danger # 4 Pension Recycling Rules

If you make larger than normal pension contributions a couple of years before you withdraw tax-free cash from your pension, there is a danger that HMRC will argue that you are recycling your tax-free lump sum.

If the recycling rules are triggered, your tax-free lump sum will be treated as an unauthorised payment, resulting in a tax charge of up to 70% (see Chapter 9).

According to HMRC, the recycling rules will also apply if, instead of funding the pension contribution directly from your tax-free lump sum, you use your available savings to pay the contribution and then use your tax-free lump sum to replenish those savings.

The recycling rules will be triggered if you always intended your tax-free lump sum to be an integral way of paying the increased pension contributions, albeit indirectly.

It's difficult to quantify the risk of triggering the recycling rules but the uncertainty alone is good enough reason to be careful of making bigger than normal pension contributions within a couple of years of withdrawing tax-free cash from your pension.

Practical Issue # 1 Maximising Higher Rate Tax Relief

Ian has to make a gross pension contribution of £61,533 to catch up with Peter. We know from Chapter 4 that to obtain the maximum higher-rate tax relief he must also have at least £61,533 of income taxed at 40%. Most people don't.

The bigger your catch-up contribution, the less likely you are to obtain the maximum higher-rate tax relief. Fortunately, there is a possible solution: Ian could spread his catch-up contributions over several tax years to maximise his higher-rate tax relief. This means he shouldn't leave it too close to retirement to make his catch-up contributions, especially if he also wants to make pension contributions out of his current income, in addition to investing his ISA savings.

Practical Issue # 2 Exceeding the Annual Allowance

The bigger your catch-up contribution, the more likely you are to exceed the annual allowance (see Chapter 2). The annual allowance is currently £60,000 but could be reduced in the years ahead.

Fortunately, it is possible to carry forward any unused annual allowance from the three previous tax years and a gross pension contribution of up to £240,000 is possible this year, provided you have sufficient relevant UK earnings and belonged to a pension scheme in each of those previous years.

Again, the best practical solution for Ian would probably be to spread his contributions over several tax years.

Practical Issue # 3 Tax Free Growth

Ian is able to catch up with Peter because he also enjoys tax-free investment growth in his ISA. If Ian's savings are taxed he will end up permanently worse off, even after he puts his savings in a pension.

In other words, if you are already making full use of your £20,000 ISA allowance with other savings, any postponed pension contributions would have to be placed in a taxed account which could leave you permanently worse off.

In summary, it is possible to put off pension saving if you don't want to tie up your money right now... but there are dangers and practical obstacles.

Chapter 20

How to Protect Your Child Benefit

Child benefit is an extremely valuable tax-free gift from the Government to parents. Those who qualify currently receive the following annual payments in 2026/27:

- £1,407 for the first child
- £931 for each subsequent child

Depending on the number of children, a family can expect to receive the following total child benefit payment:

Children	Total Child Benefit
1	£1,407
2	£2,337
3	£3,268
4	£4,199

plus £931 for each additional child

You can keep receiving child benefit until your children are 16 years of age or until age 20 if they are enrolled in 'relevant education' (the likes of GCSEs, A Levels, and NVQs to level 3, but not degree courses).

The Child Benefit Charge

When your income rises above £60,000 the family's child benefit is taken away by something called the 'high income child benefit charge'.

The child benefit charge used to kick in when the highest earner in the household had income over £50,000. Child benefit was fully withdrawn when that person's income reached £60,000.

Starting with the 2024/25 tax year, the charge is now only payable when the highest earner's income exceeds **£60,000**. Furthermore, the charge is now levied more gradually. The full charge is only payable when the highest earner's income reaches **£80,000**.

We would not be surprised if the £60,000-£80,000 income bracket where the child benefit charge applies remains frozen until at least April 2031, and possibly longer.

Thus, more and more taxpayers are likely to become further exposed to the charge, even if their income only increases with inflation.

It's important to note that, when it comes to calculating the child benefit charge, we are only interested in the spouse or partner with the highest income. The couple's total income does not matter.

If one person earns more than £60,000 the child benefit charge is payable, even if the other person earns nothing. For example, if a husband and wife each earn £50,000, no child benefit charge is payable (because neither earns more than £60,000).

But if the wife earns £30,000 and the husband earns £70,000 the child benefit charge is payable in part (because the highest earner in the household earns more than £60,000).

The previous Conservative Government promised to remove this unfairness by moving to a system based on total household income. However, the current Labour Government has stated that it will not proceed with this reform.

How the Child Benefit Charge Works

For every £200 the highest earner's income exceeds £60,000, the tax charge is 1% of the child benefit. So if the highest earner in the household has an income of £61,000, the tax charge is 5% of the child benefit.

For a household with two children this means a tax charge of £116 (£2,337 x 5%).

If the highest earner has an income of £70,000, the tax charge is 50% of the child benefit. For a household with two children this means a tax charge of £1,168.

Once the highest earner's income reaches £80,000, all the child benefit will effectively have been withdrawn.

Marginal Tax Rates

Those with income between £60,000 and £80,000 face high marginal income tax rates.

For example, let's say the highest earner's taxable income goes up from £65,000 to £66,000. They will pay £400 more income tax and a 5% child benefit charge – £70 for a household with one child. So the total tax charge on the additional £1,000 is £470 – that's a marginal tax rate of 47%.

The following are the marginal tax rates for more than one child:

2 Children	52%
3 Children	56%
4 Children	61%

You can typically add an extra 2% for national insurance, if your income is from employment or self employment. The marginal tax rates for dividends are different.

How Pension Contributions Can Help

One of the simplest ways for almost all taxpayers to reduce or avoid the child benefit charge is by making pension contributions.

The charge only applies if your 'adjusted net income' is over £60,000. Adjusted net income includes all income subject to income tax but is reduced by your gross pension contributions.

In Chapter 19 we looked at the pros and cons of postponing pension contributions. Those in the £60,000-£80,000 income bracket who are subject to the child benefit charge should be very wary of postponing pension contributions. If anything they should be making bigger than normal contributions!

By making pension contributions they can enjoy above average levels of income tax relief. Those with income in the £60,000 to £80,000 bracket enjoy three types of tax relief:

- Basic-rate relief
- Higher-rate relief
- Child benefit charge relief

The total tax relief will typically be as follows:

No. Children	Tax Relief
1	47%
2	52%
3	56%
4	61%
5	66%

Note: Assumes adjusted net income in £60,000-£80,000 bracket both before and after making the pension contribution.

The more children you have the more tax relief you will enjoy. Those with two children will enjoy over 50% tax relief. Most higher-rate taxpayers only enjoy 40% tax relief on their pension contributions.

Example

Alan has taxable income of £80,000 this year. His wife earns £40,000 and claims child benefit for three children: £3,268. On the top £10,000 slice of his income, Alan faces a £4,000 income tax bill and a child benefit charge of £1,634 (50% of the family's child benefit). Alan's £10,000 is reduced to just £4,366.

Let's focus in on that top £10,000 slice of his income and see how he can reduce the child benefit charge:

Alan personally contributes £8,000 into his pension. The taxman adds £2,000 of basic-rate tax relief, producing a gross pension contribution of £10,000. When Alan submits his tax return, he also receives £2,000 of higher-rate tax relief (£10,000 x 20%).

Furthermore, because the pension contribution reduces Alan's adjusted net income to £70,000, the child benefit charge is reduced by £1,634.

Alan therefore enjoys a total of £5,634 tax relief on his £10,000 pension contribution, i.e. 56% tax relief.

He ends up with £10,000 in his pension pot instead of £4,366 in after-tax income.

Bigger than Normal Pension Contributions

Those in the £60,000 to £80,000 income bracket should consider making bigger than normal pension contributions, especially if they expect their income to rise above £80,000 in the future or if their children are approaching the age where child benefit will be withdrawn.

Example
Gordon is a sole trader with taxable income of £80,000 this year. His wife earns £40,000 and claims child benefit for two children: £2,337. On the top £20,000 slice of his income, Gordon faces a 52% tax charge: £8,000 income tax and a child benefit charge of £2,337.

Gordon wouldn't normally make a gross pension contribution of more than £10,000 but decides to contribute £20,000 during the current tax year so that he can take advantage of the 52% tax relief available.

He could then suspend making any pension contributions next year, for example if his income rises from £80,000 to £90,000. A £10,000 pension contribution next year would attract just 40% tax relief, compared with the 52% available this year.

Much Bigger than Normal Pension Contributions

Even those with income *over* £80,000 can enjoy above average tax relief by making bigger than normal pension contributions.

Example
Colin has taxable income of £90,000 this year. His wife earns £40,000 and receives child benefit for four children: £4,199. On the top £30,000 slice of his income Colin faces a £16,199 tax charge: £12,000 income tax and a £4,199 child benefit charge.

If Colin makes a gross pension contribution of £10,000, he will enjoy 40% tax relief, just like most higher-rate taxpayers. He will not reduce the child benefit charge because his adjusted net income will not fall below £80,000.

Fortunately, his aunt Doris left him some money so Colin decides to make a much bigger than normal £30,000 gross pension contribution this year and then stop making contributions for a couple of years.

Colin's pension contribution attracts £12,000 income tax relief and, by reducing his adjusted net income to £60,000, allows him to entirely avoid the £4,199 child benefit charge. The total tax relief is £16,199 or 54% of his gross pension contribution.

Obviously the higher your income the bigger the pension contribution you have to make to get your income below £80,000 and ultimately down to £60,000. However, for some individuals, especially those with quite a few children, the tax relief may make it worthwhile.

The key tax planning point is that you shouldn't necessarily think in terms of avoiding the child benefit charge completely or permanently. For those with income close to £80,000 (or over £80,000 in some cases) it may be more practical to try to reduce the charge partly or reduce it in some tax years but not others.

Income below £60,000

With the £60,000-££80,000 income bracket likely to remain frozen until at least April 2031 more and more taxpayers are likely to become further exposed to the child benefit charge, even if their income only increases with inflation.

If you are the highest earner in the household and your income is currently close to, but below, £60,000, you may wish to consider *postponing* some of your pension contributions until your income rises above £60,000 and you can enjoy more tax relief.

Of course, you should probably not do this if it means forfeiting contributions from your employer.

Couples Pension Planning

Where one spouse or partner is in the £60,000 to £80,000 income bracket and the other has a smaller income, it may be worth considering getting the higher earner to make most of the family's pension contributions, even for just one or two tax years.

Where both income earners in the household are in the £60,000 to £80,000 bracket, the most tax-efficient strategy is to *equalise* their adjusted net incomes.

Example
Alistair earns £75,000, his wife Wilma earns £70,000. The couple want to make a combined gross pension contribution of £15,000 this year. If Alistair makes the entire contribution this will take his adjusted net income to £60,000. Wilma will then become the household's highest earner with £70,000, resulting in a 50% child benefit charge.

As far as reducing the child benefit charge is concerned, the best solution may be for Alistair to make a £10,000 gross pension contribution, with Wilma making a £5,000 gross contribution. They will then both have adjusted net income of £65,000 and pay a 25% child benefit charge.

Of course, many couples will prefer to keep things equal and make identical pension contributions, even if this does not produce the 'optimal' tax saving.

Self-Employed Pension Contributions

The taxable income of self-employed individuals (sole traders and business partners) tends to fluctuate more than that of salaried employees and even company owners.

A self-employed individual's taxable income is essentially the pre-tax profits of the business. These will vary from year to year if business conditions improve or decline or if the business owner alters the level of tax-deductible spending.

As a result, some self-employed business owners, who are also parents of qualifying children, may find themselves in the £60,000-£80,000 income bracket in some tax years but not others.

Where possible they should consider always making pension contributions in those '£60,000-£80,000' tax years, possibly contributions that are bigger than normal.

Funding Pension Contributions

Of course, many parents do not have a huge amount of spare cash to make bigger than normal pension contributions. This is where regular cash gifts from grandparents could be helpful.

Instead of putting money into a grandchild's Junior ISA or SIPP, grandparents should consider giving the cash to the parent whose income falls into the £60,000-£80,000 bracket, so that the parent can enjoy above average levels of tax relief by making additional pension contributions.

Other Considerations & Drawbacks

To maximise the tax relief on pension contributions it may be necessary to postpone or bring forward contributions or have one household member make bigger contributions than another.

Actions like these may have other consequences that need to be considered. For example, the second member of the household may not be happy about the highest earner accumulating all the retirement savings!

Postponing pension contributions may not be a good idea if this means you forfeit contributions from your employer or if higher-rate tax relief is eventually scrapped.

Chapter 21

Higher Income Earners

Income between £100,000 and £125,140

Once your income exceeds £100,000 your £12,570 income tax personal allowance is gradually taken away. It is reduced by £1 for every £2 you earn above £100,000.

For example, if your income is £110,000 your personal allowance will be reduced by £5,000.

Once your income reaches £125,140 you will have no personal allowance left at all.

Paying Tax at 60%

The effect of having your personal allowance taken away is that most people earning between £100,000 and £125,140 face a hefty marginal income tax rate of 60%.

For example, someone with a £100,000 salary who receives a £10,000 pay rise will pay 40% tax on the extra income: £4,000. They'll also have their personal allowance reduced by £5,000, which means £5,000 of income that was previously tax free will effectively be taxed at 40%. Total extra tax: £6,000 which is 60%.

Saving Tax at 60%

The flipside of this is that anyone in the £100,000-£125,140 income bracket who makes pension contributions can enjoy 60% tax relief.

Your personal allowance is reduced if your 'adjusted net income' is more than £100,000. When calculating your adjusted net income you usually deduct any pension contributions you have made.

Example
Tilly has taxable income of £110,000 and invests £8,000 in her pension. She will receive a £2,000 top up from the taxman (her basic-rate tax relief), resulting in a gross pension contribution of £10,000. She will also receive higher-rate tax relief of £2,000 (£10,000 x 20%).

In addition, by making a gross pension of £10,000 her adjusted net income will be reduced from £110,000 to £100,000, so none of her personal allowance will be taken away. Additional tax saving: £2,000 (£5,000 x 40%).

In summary, her £10,000 gross pension contribution produces £6,000 of tax savings – a total of 60% tax relief.

The £100,000 Childcare Trap

Once your adjusted net income exceeds £100,000 you also lose your entitlement to various childcare benefits including:

- Free Childcare for Working Parents
- Tax-free Childcare

These benefits are extremely valuable, often worth many thousands of pounds per year per child.

£100,000 acts as a cliff edge – if either parent earns £1 more than £100,000 the family will lose these benefits completely.

Fortunately, pension contributions reduce your adjusted net income and can therefore help you hold onto your childcare entitlement. The key is to make gross pension contributions big enough to bring your adjusted net income down below £100,000.

For the remainder of this chapter we will be focusing solely on the income tax benefits of making pension contributions when your income is close to or exceeds £100,000.

However, those affected by the childcare cliff edge have a far greater incentive to manage their pension contributions carefully – ensuring, where possible, that their adjusted net income does not exceed £100,000 for as many years as necessary.

Maximising 60% Tax Relief

Those with income between £100,000 and £125,140 may wish to consider making *bigger than normal* contributions while they remain in this heavily taxed bracket (or slightly above it).

For example, someone who has taxable income of £115,000 can make a gross pension contribution of up £15,000 with 60% tax relief.

Someone who has taxable income of £125,000 can make a gross pension contribution of up £25,000 with 60% tax relief.

These contributions may be more than they are willing to make but could be worth considering (resources allowing) if they expect their income to keep rising.

This is because, once your income rises above £125,140, your personal allowance will have been fully withdrawn and you will become an additional-rate taxpayer. You will then only enjoy 45% tax relief on some of your pension contributions.

For example, someone who has taxable income of £125,000 this year may see it rise to, say, £140,000 in a few years' time. The first £14,860 of their gross pension contributions (£140,000 – £125,140) will then attract just 45% tax relief.

Only by making a contribution bigger than £14,860 will they be able to enjoy any tax relief at 60%. For example, someone with taxable income of £140,000 can make a gross pension contribution of £14,860 with 45% tax relief and a further contribution of up to £25,140 with 60% tax relief.

The further your income rises above £125,140, the harder it is to make pension contributions big enough to enjoy not just 45% tax relief, but 60% as well.

Thus, making bigger than normal pension contributions while your income is still in the £100,000-£125,140 tax bracket (or only a little over it) may be worth considering.

Pension Contributions that Are Too Big

Those with income between £100,000 and £125,140 should also be careful about making pension contributions that are "too big".

If Tilly in the above example makes a gross pension contribution of more than £10,000 she will only enjoy 40% tax relief on the additional pension contribution.

This is because a contribution of just £10,000 is enough to fully recover her income tax personal allowance.

Similarly, someone with taxable income of £120,000 can make a gross pension contribution of £20,000 this year and enjoy 60% tax relief.

But if they make a pension contribution of £25,000 they will enjoy just 40% tax relief on the final £5,000 of the contribution.

In other words it is less attractive, from a tax saving standpoint, to put money in a pension that will enjoy just 40% tax relief this year if you can enjoy 60% tax relief by putting the same money in your pension next year.

Income Close to £100,000

What if your taxable income is currently less than £100,000 but you expect to be earning more than £100,000 in the near future?

The £100,000 threshold has never been increased since it was introduced in April 2010. If it had gone up with inflation you would only start losing your personal allowance with an income of over £180,000 today.

Because the £100,000 threshold does not increase with inflation there's a good chance someone who currently earns less than £100,000 will lose some of their personal allowance in the future.

For example, if you're currently earning £90,000 there's a good chance your income will exceed £100,000 in a few years' time, even if your income only increases because of inflation.

Or take the example of a self-employed person who currently earns £75,000 with a business that is growing by around 20% per year. There's a good chance that person will be earning over £100,000 in a couple of years' time.

What are the tax planning implications?

Those who are currently earning less than £100,000 but expect to be earning more than £100,000 in the near future may wish to consider postponing some of their pension contributions until they are in the £100,000 to £125,140 income bracket.

Pension contributions made in this income bracket will enjoy 60% tax relief instead of the normal 40% tax relief enjoyed by higher-rate taxpayers.

Of course, when it comes to postponing pension contributions all the normal caveats apply and many have been mentioned in previous chapters.

For example, reducing your pension contributions may not be a good idea if it means losing out on contributions from your employer. Pension tax relief could be made less generous in the future or there could be other tax changes that undo any such planning.

Income over £125,140

When your income rises above £125,140 you become an additional-rate taxpayer and start paying 45% tax on most types of income.

The flipside is you can enjoy 45% tax relief on your pension contributions.

Those on higher incomes will thus generally enjoy tax relief as follows on their pension contributions:

- £50,270-£100,000 40% tax relief
- £100,000-£125,140 60% tax relief
- £125,140 or more 45% tax relief

The additional-rate threshold was £150,000 for many years but was reduced to £125,140 on 6th April 2023.

If the original £150,000 threshold had instead gone up with inflation, you would only start paying 45% tax with an income of around £275,000 today – over TWICE the current threshold!

There are probably lots of people who are currently additional-rate taxpayers but would never have expected to be in this tax bracket when the additional rate was introduced back in April 2010.

How is Additional-Rate Relief Calculated?

If you are an additional-rate taxpayer the extra tax relief on your pension contributions is typically given by extending both your basic-rate band and higher-rate band by the amount of your gross pension contributions.

This means more of your income will be taxed at 20% instead of 40% and more of your income will be taxed at 40% instead of 45%.

Example

Jake is a sole trader with pre-tax profits of £140,000. If he doesn't make any pension contributions he will have £14,860 of income taxed at 45% (£140,000 - £125,140).

He personally invests £8,000 in his pension. The taxman adds £2,000 of basic-rate relief for a gross contribution of £10,000 (£8,000/0.8).

His basic-rate band will therefore be increased by £10,000, allowing £10,000 of his income to be taxed at 20% instead of 40%. This saves Jake £2,000 in tax (£10,000 x 20%).

His higher-rate band will also be increased by £10,000, allowing £10,000 of his income to be taxed at 40% instead of 45%. This saves Jake an additional £500 in tax (£10,000 x 5%).

His total tax relief is £4,500 which is 45% of his £10,000 gross pension contribution.

Jake can make a gross pension contribution of up to £14,860 with 45% tax relief.

But what if he makes a pension contribution of more than £14,860 – will he enjoy less tax relief? No, he will start enjoying 60% tax relief because the additional contribution will take his adjusted net income below £125,140, which means he will recover some of his income tax personal allowance.

This is one of the major differences between higher-rate taxpayers and additional-rate taxpayers.

In Chapter 4 we saw that higher-rate taxpayers will start receiving just 20% tax relief if their pension contributions are "too big" and exceed the amount of income they have taxed at 40%.

Additional-rate taxpayers can enjoy a combination of 45% tax relief and 60% tax relief if their pension contributions are big enough, as we shall see in the next section.

Enjoying 45% <u>and</u> 60% Tax Relief

Additional-rate taxpayers with income that is not significantly higher than £125,140 may be able to enjoy 60% tax relief on some of their pension contributions.

Example Revisited

Jake is a sole trader with pre-tax profits of £140,000. He has £14,860 of income taxed at 45% (£140,000 - £125,140).

He decides to make a bigger than normal pension contribution of £32,000. The taxman adds £8,000 of basic-rate relief for a gross contribution of £40,000 (£32,000/0.8).

The £40,000 gross pension contribution will reduce his adjusted net income from £140,000 to £100,000, which means none of his income tax personal allowance will be taken away. This saves Jake £5,028 in income tax (£12,570 x 40%).

His basic-rate band is increased by £40,000, allowing £40,000 of his income to be taxed at 20% instead of 40%. This saves Jake £8,000 in income tax (£40,000 x 20%).

His higher-rate band is also increased by £40,000, allowing up to £40,000 of his income to be taxed at 40% instead of 45%, i.e. a saving of 5%. As it happens Jake only has £14,860 of income taxed at 45% so the additional saving is £743 (£14,860 x 5%).

His total tax relief is £21,771 (£8,000 + £5,028 + £8,000 + £743) which is 54.4% of his £40,000 gross pension contribution.

What this example shows is that anyone who has taxable income of more than £125,140 can potentially enjoy overall tax relief of more than 45% by making a gross pension contribution that is big enough to take their adjusted net income back down into the £100,000-£125,140 bracket.

Shortcut Calculation

Jake's total tax relief on his £40,000 gross pension contribution can be calculated quickly as follows:

£14,860 x 45% + £25,140 x 60% = £21,771

He enjoys 45% tax relief on the amount by which his income exceeds the additional-rate threshold (£14,860).

He enjoys 60% tax relief on the remainder which falls into the £100,000-£125,140 tax bracket.

His tax relief percentage is 54.4% (£21,771/£40,000).

In this example Jake makes a pension contribution big enough to take his adjusted net income all the way down to £100,000, so he is able to claw back ALL of his personal allowance.

But what if Jake can only afford a gross pension contribution of £20,000? This will reduce his adjusted net income from £140,000 to £120,000 which means he will recover some, but not all, of his personal allowance.

His total tax relief will be:

£14,860 x 45% + £5,140 x 60% = £9,771

Again £14,860 is simply the amount by which his income exceeds the additional-rate threshold and £5,140 is simply the rest of his pension contribution.

Jake's tax relief percentage will be 48.9% (£9,771/£20,000).

In summary, an additional-rate taxpayer can enjoy tax relief of between 45% and 60% by making a gross pension contribution that is big enough to take their adjusted net income into the £100,000-£125,140 bracket.

Table 5 shows the total tax relief that can be enjoyed by a variety of high income earners.

It's assumed the individuals have enough "earnings" to make these pension contributions. Earnings are not the same as taxable income (earnings typically include salary income or profits from self employment – see Chapter 2).

It's also assumed that the annual gross contribution is no more than £60,000, the new annual allowance from 6th April 2023. Higher contributions may be possible when the individual has unused annual allowance from the three previous tax years.

Table 5
High Income Earners Tax Relief

Taxable Income	£10k	£20k	£30k	£40k	£50k	£60k
	Gross Pension Contribution					
£100,000	40%	40%	40%	40%	40%	37%
£110,000	60%	50%	47%	45%	44%	43%
£120,000	60%	60%	53%	50%	48%	47%
£130,000	53%	56%	58%	53%	51%	49%
£140,000	45%	49%	53%	54%	52%	50%
£150,000	45%	45%	48%	51%	53%	50%
£160,000	45%	45%	45%	47%	50%	51%
£170,000	45%	45%	45%	45%	47%	49%
£180,000	45%	45%	45%	45%	45%	46%
£190,000	45%	45%	45%	45%	45%	45%
£200,000	45%	45%	45%	45%	45%	45%

Tax Planning Implications

The tax relief in the table varies significantly from 37% to 60%.

If you make pension contributions when your income is "too high" you may only enjoy 45% tax relief. This is because even a big contribution may not be enough to reduce your adjusted net income much below £125,140, where you will enjoy 60% tax relief.

For example, someone with taxable income of £180,000 who makes a gross pension contribution of £60,000 will enjoy 45% tax relief on the first £54,860 and 60% on just £5,140 – a total of 46% tax relief.

Arguably the best time to make pension contributions is when your income is in the £100,000-£125,140 income bracket (where tax relief of 60% is available) or just a bit higher than £125,140 (where overall tax relief of almost 60% is available).

For example, someone with taxable income of £130,000 who makes a gross pension contribution of £30,000 will enjoy 58% tax relief, which is a very good outcome.

It may indeed be attractive, from a tax saving perspective, to make bigger than normal contributions before your income rises significantly higher than £125,140 in order to make the most of the higher tax relief that is available.

In other words, you should try to make contributions which enjoy 60% tax relief instead of 45% tax relief.

However, if your income is in the £100,000-£125,140 bracket or a bit higher it's also important not to make a pension contribution that is "too big", if maximizing tax relief is the priority.

For example, someone with taxable income of £110,000 who makes a gross pension contribution of £60,000 will enjoy just 43% tax relief. They'll enjoy 60% tax relief on the first £10,000, 40% on the next £49,730 and just 20% on the final £270 – a total of 43% tax relief.

Postponing Pension Contributions

From a tax saving perspective, additional-rate taxpayers may wish to consider making bigger than normal pension contributions in some tax years and smaller than normal contributions in other tax years.

This way they may be able to enjoy 60% tax relief instead of 45% tax relief on more of their contributions.

Take the example of someone who has taxable income of £160,000 and normally makes a gross pension contribution of £30,000 per year. A pension contribution of £30,000 will enjoy just 45% tax relief.

However, if that person makes a contribution of £60,000 in year 1 and no contribution in year 2 they will enjoy a total of 51% tax relief.

Of course, when it comes to postponing or halting pension contributions all the normal caveats apply, as mentioned earlier in this chapter.

The Tapered Annual Allowance

Some high earners taxpayers face restrictions to their pension contributions. The annual allowance can be reduced from £60,000 to just £10,000. Fortunately, the so-called pension taper now kicks in at much higher income levels than previously. As a result, many high earners can enjoy higher pension contributions than before.

Threshold Income

The first thing you have to calculate is your 'threshold income'. If your threshold income is £200,000 or less you are exempt from tapering and can make pension contributions just like anyone else.

Your threshold income is, broadly speaking, your total taxable income. This includes your salary, self-employment profits, dividends, rental profits, interest income and any other taxable income you receive.

From this you deduct any pension contributions you have made *personally* (you deduct the gross contributions).

You can also deduct other reliefs listed in Section 24 of the Income Tax Act 2007. These include things like trade loss relief.

Employer pension contributions are ignored when calculating threshold income. But you must add back any salary sacrificed in exchange for employer pension contributions if this arrangement was set up after 8th July 2015.

The threshold used to be £110,000 but was increased to £200,000 on 6th April 2020.

Example 1
Dirk is self-employed and has taxable income of £250,000 this year (coming mostly from his business and some rental properties). He makes a gross pension contribution of £60,000 into his SIPP (he invests £48,000 personally and the taxman tops this up with £12,000).

His gross pension contribution is deducted from his taxable income, giving him a threshold income of £190,000. Because Dirk's threshold income is less than £200,000, he is completely unaffected by the tapered annual allowance. This means his annual allowance for the current tax year (his permitted pension contribution) is £60,000.

Example 2

Beric is a company owner and pays himself salary and dividend income totalling £200,000. He also has taxable rental profits of £70,000, so his total taxable income is £270,000.

His company makes a pension contribution of £50,000 for him (an employer contribution) but we ignore this when calculating his threshold income. He doesn't make any pension contributions personally.

Beric's threshold income is therefore £270,000. Because this exceeds £200,000, he is potentially affected by the tapered annual allowance.

Adjusted Income

If your threshold income exceeds £200,000 the next thing you have to calculate is your 'adjusted income'. Broadly speaking, your adjusted income is your total taxable income *plus* any pension contributions made by your employer.

You also add back any contributions to an occupational pension scheme under a net pay arrangement (where your contributions are deducted from your salary before calculating PAYE).

You can also deduct the reliefs listed in Section 24 of the Income Tax Act 2007.

Your annual allowance will only be reduced if your adjusted income exceeds £260,000. The annual allowance is reduced by £1 for every £2 your adjusted income exceeds £260,000.

So an individual with adjusted income of £290,000 will have their annual allowance reduced by £15,000 (£30,000/2), giving them an annual allowance of £45,000.

Your annual allowance cannot fall below £10,000 – this is what's known as the "minimum tapered annual allowance".

The tapered annual allowance used to be £4,000 but was increased to £10,000 on 6th April 2023. At the same time, the adjusted income limit was increased from £240,000 to £260,000.

Pension contributions that exceed the tapered annual allowance face the annual allowance charge. The excess contributions will be added to your income and taxed.

If the charge exceeds £2,000 it may be possible to have it paid out of your pension savings. This may only be possible if total contributions to the scheme in question exceed the standard annual allowance (£60,000).

Example 2 continued
As we saw earlier, Beric has total taxable income of £270,000 and his company makes a contribution of £50,000 on his behalf.

Beric's adjusted income is £320,000: £270,000 + £50,000

His annual allowance is reduced by £30,000: (£320,000 - £260,000)/2

His annual allowance is therefore £30,000: £60,000 - £30,000

Beric faces an annual allowance charge on £20,000:

£50,000 - £30,000 = £20,000

Calculating the Tapered Annual Allowance in Practice

Beric can avoid the charge by getting his company to make a smaller pension contribution (no more than £36,666).

Alternatively, he may be able to extract less income from his company (no more than £160,000) to ensure his total taxable income reduces to £230,000 and he is able to benefit from a tapered annual allowance of £50,000.

Company owners may find it easier than others to control their taxable income to reduce their threshold income and adjusted income. But they may have to be wary of triggering a special tax anti-avoidance rule (see below).

Most regular salaried employees will find it fairly easy to calculate their adjusted income and threshold income. So too will company owners who pay themselves a set amount of salary and dividend income.

Problems may arise where the taxpayer has income that is less predictable, for example profits from self employment or rental profits from property. In these circumstances it may not be possible to calculate how much taxable income you have (and thus your tapered annual allowance) until *after* the tax year has ended. By then it will be too late to make pension contributions.

Those who wish to benefit from pension contributions and think they are affected by the tapered annual allowance may need to estimate their taxable income just *before* the end of the tax year.

The Tapered Annual Allowance and Carry Forward

All is not lost if your pension contributions exceed your tapered annual allowance. You can still carry forward any unused annual allowance from the three previous tax years. (The amount you can carry forward is your unused tapered annual allowance from each of those years).

Carry forward could be a lifeline if your contributions accidentally exceed the tapered annual allowance. Beric in the above example will avoid the annual allowance charge if he has at least £20,000 of unused annual allowance from the three previous tax years.

Anti-Avoidance Rule

An anti-avoidance rule is in place to prevent anyone entering into an arrangement which involves reducing their adjusted or threshold income and increasing their income in a different tax year. The anti-avoidance provisions apply when it is reasonable to assume that the main purpose, or one of the main purposes of the arrangement, is to reduce the impact of the tapered annual allowance. If the anti-avoidance provisions apply, then the relevant arrangement will be ignored for the purposes of calculating the tapered annual allowance.

It is unclear how this measure could be applied to individuals such as company owners who vary their income from year to year.

Maximum Pension Contribution

The £200,000 threshold income limit and £260,000 adjusted income limit were significantly lower a few years ago. Many high earners are now unaffected by the tapered annual allowance and can make fairly big pension contributions with full tax relief.

For example, anyone with a taxable income of up to £260,000 can personally contribute up to £60,000 to a pension every year (assuming there are no employer contributions). The following table shows how much high earners can personally contribute at different income levels:

Taxable income	Maximum pension contribution*
Up to £260,000	£60,000
£270,000	£55,000
£280,000	£50,000
£290,000	£45,000
£300,000	£40,000
£310,000	£35,000
£320,000	£30,000
£330,000	£25,000
£340,000	£20,000
£350,000	£15,000
£360,000+	£10,000

* Maximum gross contribution that can be paid personally. Assumes there is no employer contribution. Ignores carry forward from 3 previous tax years.

Maximum Contributions – Company Owners

A company owner with taxable income of up to £200,000 can get their company to make a pension contribution of up to £60,000 per year with full tax relief. The following table shows how much the company can contribute at different income levels:

Taxable Income	Maximum Company Pension Contribution*
Up to £200,000	£60,000
£215,000	£55,000
£230,000	£50,000
£245,000	£45,000
£260,000	£40,000
£275,000	£35,000
£290,000	£30,000
£305,000	£25,000
£320,000	£20,000
£335,000	£15,000
£350,000+	£10,000

* Assumes there is no contribution by the company owner personally. Ignores potential carry forward from 3 previous tax years

Planning under the Tapered Annual Allowance

Some high income earners may be comfortable with a reduced annual allowance. For example, a sole trader with profits of £280,000, who makes regular pension contributions of £40,000 per year, may be quite happy with an annual allowance of £50,000.

However, if you expect your income to increase, resulting in further reductions in your annual allowance, it may be desirable to make bigger pension contributions now, while you can. In other words, it may be better to contribute £50,000 now instead of £40,000.

Some individuals whose threshold income is *below* £200,000 at present may also wish to speed up their pension contributions at present if they expect to be earning well over £200,000 in a few years' time.

It may also be possible to mitigate the damage caused by the tapered annual allowance by getting your spouse to make bigger pension contributions, even if these only attract 40% tax relief.

Example
Miriam is a self-employed solicitor with profits of £330,000. Her husband Nick earns £125,000. During the current tax year Miriam would like to make a pension contribution of £60,000 but is restricted to £25,000. Nick normally makes a contribution of £25,000 per year and enjoys 60% tax relief (as explained earlier in this chapter).

The couple therefore decide to swap the amounts they contribute: Nick contributes £60,000 per year (using the couple's shared resources) and Miriam contributes £25,000.

Nick's additional pension contribution of £35,000 will only attract 40% tax relief, compared with Miriam's 45%, however the total loss of tax relief is just £1,750 (£35,000 x 5%).

For this strategy to work it is essential that Nick has sufficient income taxed at 40% so that all of the additional contribution attracts higher-rate tax relief (see Chapter 4). It may also be important that Nick's higher contributions do not result in him building such a big pension pot that a lot of his pension income is eventually taxed at 40% instead of the 20% basic rate of income tax.

Part 5

Employees

Chapter 22

Auto-Enrolment: The Advent of Compulsory Pensions

"Currently 14 million people get no contribution from their employer towards a pension."

Former Secretary of State for Work and Pensions, Yvette Cooper, January 2010

To address this problem, compulsory workplace pensions were introduced. Known as 'auto enrolment' it forces all employers to enrol nearly all their staff into a workplace pension.

Exemptions

Only employees earning more than £10,000 and aged from 22 to state pension age need to be *automatically* enrolled into a pension. However, some older and younger employees and those who earn less than £10,000 also have workplace pension rights:

- If an employee earns less than £6,240 in 2026/27 they don't need to be automatically enrolled but the employer has to give them access to a pension if they request it and if they are aged between 16 and 74. However, the employer is not required to contribute.

- If an employee earns between £6,240 and £10,000 and their age is between 16 and 74 they don't need to be automatically enrolled but do have the right to opt in. If they do decide to join the pension scheme the employer will have to contribute as well.

- If an employee earns more than £10,000 but is aged 16-21 or between state pension age and 74 they don't need to be automatically enrolled but do have the right to opt in. If they do decide to join the pension scheme the employer will have to contribute as well.

Company Directors

According to the Pension Regulator a company does not have any automatic-enrolment duties when:

- It has just one director, with no other staff
- It has a number of directors, none of whom has an employment contract, with no other staff
- It has a number of directors, only one of whom has an employment contract, with no other staff

A contract of employment does not have to be in writing. However, according to the Pension Regulator, if there is no written contract of employment, or other evidence of an intention to create an employer/worker relationship between the company and the director, it will not argue that an employment contract exists.

If a director does not have an employment contract they do not need to be assessed for automatic enrolment.

If a director has a contract of employment and is not the only person working for the company under an employment contract, they are not exempt. Depending on their age and earnings, they may then qualify for automatic enrolment.

However, unlike other employees, the company may choose not to enrol a director who qualifies for automatic enrolment. If the company chooses not to enrol the director, the director still has the right to opt in or join a pension.

If the company decides not to enrol an employed director who is eligible for automatic enrolment, and it has no other eligible staff, it does not have to set up a pension scheme.

However, it will need to make a 'declaration of compliance'.

The Contributions

Employers are forced to make a minimum pension contribution and, in practice, so too are most employees.

Generally speaking, contributions are a percentage of 'qualifying earnings'.

The total minimum contribution is 8% with at least 3% coming from the employer.

The total minimum contribution can be paid by the employer but in practice many small firms will insist that the employee makes up the required balance.

This means that many employees are forced to contribute 5% to a pension if they want to benefit from a 3% contribution from their employer.

Employees' contributions enjoy tax relief as normal, which means 4% will come from them personally and the extra 1% will be added by the taxman in the form of basic-rate tax relief.

Qualifying Earnings

The minimum contributions are generally not based on the employee's total earnings but rather on a band of earnings.

The lower and upper thresholds for 2026/27 are £6,240 and £50,270 respectively. What this means is that pension contributions are typically based on earnings of up to £44,030 (£50,270 - £6,240).

For example, someone with employment income of £60,000 will have their pension contributions based on earnings of £44,030. Someone with employment income of £20,000 will have their pension contributions based on earnings of £13,760 (£20,000 minus £6,240).

Opting out

Employees will be automatically enrolled but can opt out if they wish by completing an opt-out notice. Employers are, however, required to automatically re-enrol eligible employees back into the workplace pension scheme roughly every three years.

No doubt some employees, especially younger employees, will prefer to opt out if they are compelled by their employers to make a pension contribution of up to 5%.

How Valuable is Auto Enrolment?

The answer to this question probably depends on whether you are an employee or employer.

Many small business owners cannot afford to save for their own retirement, let alone those of their entire workforce!

And this, perhaps, is the crucial point. If your employer has been dragged kicking and screaming into a system of compulsory pensions, you may end up being paid less to cover the cost. For example, future pay increases may be reduced. This is basic economics.

Even an 8% pension contribution is not big enough to solve most people's retirement saving problem, especially since it will typically be based on a small band of the employee's earnings.

For example, let's say you currently earn £65,000 and you and your employer make a combined 8% pension contribution for 20 years based on the £44,030 band of qualifying earnings, with all amounts increased to take account of inflation.

After 20 years the pension pot will be worth around £180,000, if the investments in the fund grow by, say, 7% per year. That's a fairly decent amount BUT insignificant in terms of providing you with a meaningful retirement income.

In 20 years' time your salary may have grown to around £95,000, so the money paid into your pension pot will be worth less than two years' salary – not exactly enough for a golden retirement!

This does not mean that you should opt out of auto-enrolment. That would mean forfeiting the pension contribution your employer makes, which could arguably be regarded as free money.

What it does mean is that those who are making the minimum pension contribution under auto enrolment will almost certainly need to build additional retirement savings, either using pensions or other savings products.

Chapter 23

Free Cash from Employers

As we know from the previous chapter, many individuals enjoy more than just tax relief on their pension contributions. They also receive 'free' money from their employers.

Many company pension schemes offer far more generous employer contributions than those required under the auto-enrolment rules. Some employees receive employer contributions totalling 5%-10% of their salary, provided they contribute a similar amount. With the help of employer pension contributions, you may be able to save twice as quickly as you could on your own.

Sometimes employers will double what you put in. For example, in one pension scheme I know about, the company puts in 12% if the employee puts in 6%.

Many employees recognize that giving up any of this free money (by not contributing at all or not contributing enough) is tantamount to looking a gift horse in the mouth.

I remember listening on the radio to a woman describe how she and her husband were trying to cut out every single bit of frivolous spending so that they could contribute as much as possible to her husband's workplace pension scheme, thereby enjoying a hefty matching contribution from the employer.

She described it as "austerity today for prosperity tomorrow".

Not everyone has been as financially prudent as this couple. According to Standard Life, before the advent of auto-enrolment employers were offering a contribution to around 10 million employees but around 4.5 million did not sign up to their employer's pension scheme.

These employees were missing out on a total of nearly £6 billion per year of free money!

Not surprisingly in the past it has been younger employees who have contributed the least to pensions. According to the Department for Work and Pensions, in 2011 only 15% of employees aged 16-24 participated in workplace pension schemes, whereas pension participation was 58% in the 45-54 age group.

Millions more people now belong to a workplace pension thanks to the introduction of compulsory pensions BUT some employees (such as younger employees) may opt out.

I'm not in the business of criticising the savings habits of others, especially those who have children to support. Many families have very little income left after paying extortionate amounts of tax and after paying down debts like student loans and home mortgages.

Nevertheless, if there is ever a good time to contribute to a pension it's when your employer is offering you money on a plate.

Example

Douglas is an employee with a salary of £60,000 per year. Let's say his employer offers to make a 5% pension contribution, with Douglas contributing 5% personally.

If Douglas decides to opt out of his workplace pension scheme, he will have additional income of £3,000 (£60,000 x 5%). After paying income tax he will be left with £1,800 (ignoring national insurance).

Alternatively, if Douglas decides to join his workplace pension scheme he will end up with £6,000 sitting in his pension (£3,000 contributed personally and £3,000 from his employer).

Douglas has to decide whether £1,800 of income today is more valuable than £6,000 tucked away until he retires.

This is just a snapshot from a single year. Douglas will lose £4,200 (£6,000 - £1,800) every year he is not a member of his employer's pension scheme. Furthermore, he will also lose the tax-free growth on that money.

If a 25-year-old decides to forego a pension contribution from his employer he will lose possibly 40 years of tax-free compound growth. On next year's foregone contribution he will lose 39 years of tax-free growth... and so on.

So how much do you stand to lose over the long term by not receiving pension contributions from your employer?

Example continued

Let's say Douglas opts out of his workplace pension scheme for five years and therefore loses out on five years of employer contributions (at 5% of his salary).

We'll assume his salary increases by 3% per year, which means the contributions from his employer will also grow by 3% per year. We'll also assume the money in his pension grows by 7% per year tax free.

Douglas loses out on the following employer contributions over the five-year period: £3,000, £3,090, £3,183, £3,278 and £3,377. When you add tax-free compound growth at 7% per year, the total value of the employer pension contributions after five years is £19,523.

However, that's not the end of the story. Depending on how far away Douglas is from retirement he could lose out on tax-free growth on this money for possibly another 10, 20, 30 or even 40 years. For example, those five years' worth of contributions will be worth £27,382 after 10 years, £53,865 after 20 years, £105,960 after 30 years and £208,439 after 40 years.

Remember, all we are looking at here are the contributions that would be made by Douglas's employer (the 'free money'). We are ignoring the contributions that he would make personally and on which he would enjoy full income tax relief.

The top half of Table 6 shows exactly the same thing for a range of different starting salaries. In each case we assume the salary grows by 3% per year, the employer makes a 5% pension contribution for five years and the money grows by 7% per year tax free.

For example, if your salary is £30,000 now and you lose out on five years' worth of employer contributions and an additional 15 years of tax-free growth on that money, the total loss to your pension pot after 20 years will be £26,932.

The second half of the table shows exactly the same thing except this time we assume the employee is not a member of the workplace pension scheme for 10 years. For example, if your salary is £30,000 now and you lose out on 10 years' worth of employer contributions and an additional 10 years of tax-free growth on that money, the total loss to your pension pot after 20 years will be £49,193.

Table 6
5% Employer Pension Contribution
Long-term Value

Employer Contributions for 5 Years
Value after...

Starting Salary £	10 Years £	20 Years £	30 Years £	40 Years £
20,000	9127	17,955	35,320	69,480
30,000	13,691	26,932	52,980	104,220
40,000	18,255	35,910	70,640	138,959
50,000	22,818	44,887	88,300	173,699
60,000	27,382	53,865	105,960	208,439
70,000	31,946	62,842	123,620	243,179
80,000	36,509	71,820	141,280	277,919
90,000	41,073	80,797	158,940	312,659
100,000	45,637	89,774	176,600	347,399

Employer Contributions for 10 Years
Value after...

Starting Salary £	10 Years £	20 Years £	30 Years £	40 Years £
20,000	16,672	32,795	64,514	126,908
30,000	25,007	49,193	96,770	190,362
40,000	33,343	65,591	129,027	253,816
50,000	41,679	81,989	161,284	317,270
60,000	50,015	98,386	193,541	380,724
70,000	58,350	114,784	225,798	444,178
80,000	66,686	131,182	258,054	507,632
90,000	75,022	147,579	290,311	571,086
100,000	83,358	163,977	322,568	634,540

Different Employer Pension Contributions

Different employers pay different amounts into their employees' pensions. To find out how much a bigger or smaller employer contribution is worth all you have to do is scale the numbers in Table 6 up or down.

For example, if the employer offers a 10% contribution you simply double the numbers. In this case Douglas, with a starting salary of £60,000 and no contributions for five years, will have lost £107,730 after 20 years (£53,865 x 2).

If the employer offers an 8% contribution you multiply the numbers by 1.6 (found by dividing 8 by 5).

If the employer offers a 3% contribution you multiply the numbers by 0.6 (found by dividing 3 by 5).

... and so on.

Putting Things in Perspective

The numbers in the table are quite large and imply that, by not belonging to a workplace pension scheme, and not receiving pension contributions from your employer, you may be losing a lot of free money.

However, it's important to put the figures in perspective. Let's say Douglas is 35 years old and 30 years away from retirement. By not receiving employer pension contributions for five years, his pension pot will have lost £105,960 of free money after 30 years. However, by that time his salary will have grown to £141,394 (growing at just 3% per year). What this means is that not contributing to his employer's pension for five years has cost him around nine months' salary.

Is this a price worth paying? Only Douglas can answer that.

And what if Douglas is a high flier and his pay increases by more than inflation, as he climbs the corporate ladder?
If we assume his salary grows by 7% per year we find that after 30 years he is sitting on a salary of £426,855. And his pension pot will have lost out on £114,184 worth of employer contributions.

In total Douglas will have lost just over three months' pay by not receiving pension contributions from his employer for five years.

Personally, I am of the opinion that anyone offered free cash by their employer should grasp the opportunity with open arms.

BUT...

If you do not belong to your workplace pension scheme for just a few years, this may not have a significant effect on your income in retirement IF you expect your salary to grow rapidly, resulting in bigger employer pension contributions in later years.

Chapter 24

Salary Sacrifice Pensions

In a traditional company pension scheme, the employee makes a pension contribution personally out of their salary and the employer makes a contribution too.

Although employees obtain income tax relief on the amount they contribute personally, they still have to pay national insurance, as do their employers.

For basic-rate taxpayers as much as £230 of national insurance is payable by the employee and employer on every £1,000 of salary used to make pension contributions (8% paid by the employee and 15% by the employer).

For higher or additional-rate taxpayers, as much as £170 is payable (2% by the employee and 15% by the employer).

With salary sacrifice pensions, the employee stops making pension contributions personally and gives up some of their salary in return for a bigger pension contribution from their employer.

Because employer pension contributions are exempt from national insurance this saves both the employee and employer from having to pay national insurance on the amount of salary sacrificed.

In some salary sacrifice pension schemes, the employer pays some or all of their own national insurance saving into the employee's pension pot, which can lead to a significant increase in the amount contributed.

In other words, salary sacrifice pensions allow you to enjoy full income tax AND national insurance relief on your pension contributions (most pension contributions only enjoy income tax relief, not national insurance relief).

For example, a basic rate taxpayer who is making a gross pension contribution of £1,250 personally could see this increase to £1,597 (an increase of 28%) under a salary sacrifice arrangement: with no reduction in their take-home pay.

A higher-rate taxpayer who is making a gross pension contribution of, say, £3,000 personally could see this increase to £3,568 (an increase of 19%) under a salary sacrifice arrangement, again with no reduction in their take-home pay.

This is assuming the employer pays their own national insurance saving into the employee's pension pot. If you are a higher rate taxpayer (paying just 2% national insurance), a salary sacrifice arrangement will not leave you much better off unless your employer also agrees to pass on some or all of their much higher 15% saving.

Salary sacrifice also delivers immediate tax relief, avoiding the need for higher-rate employees to claim higher-rate tax relief later.

It's important to point out that salary sacrifice must be a *contractual agreement*, not an informal arrangement between the employee and employer. Some of the earnings to which the employee has a right are given up in exchange for an employer pension contribution.

It's essential to get some professional help when implementing a salary sacrifice pension arrangement because you have to get the "paperwork" right.

Salary sacrifice pensions are used by some of the country's biggest companies and universities, including BT, Tesco and the BBC.

Changes Ahead

As announced in the November 2025 Budget, the Government is placing a £2,000 cap on the amount of salary sacrifice pension contributions exempt from national insurance.

The good news is the cap will only come into force on **6th April 2029**, so there is still quite a lot of time left to make use of this powerful tax break.

Although the implementation date is some way off, we do expect the change to go ahead: at the time of writing the legislation had just passed its second reading in the House of Lords.

Table 7
Effect of the £2,000 Cap
Employee Sacrifices 5% Salary

Base Salary	Employee NI Saving	Employer NI Saving	Extra Employee NI	Extra Employer NI
£40,000	£160	£300	£0	£0
£45,000	£180	£338	£20	£38
£50,000	£200	£375	£40	£75
£75,000	£75	£563	£35	£263
£100,000	£100	£750	£60	£450
£125,000	£125	£938	£85	£638
£150,000	£150	£1,125	£110	£825

Employees and employers will pay national insurance on the amount of salary sacrificed above £2,000: the excess over £2,000 will be treated as ordinary employee pension contributions.

The first £2,000 will remain exempt, as will any ordinary employer contributions unrelated to the salary sacrificed.

For example, if the pension contribution under salary sacrifice is £5,000, then £3,000 will become subject to national insurance.

Although salary sacrifice pensions will become less attractive than they are at present, it's important to point out that they will still be more attractive than ordinary pension arrangements that enjoy no national insurance savings.

HMRC have also confirmed that salary sacrifice will continue to be effective for the purposes of keeping your personal allowance, tax-free childcare and child benefit (pension contributions reduce your adjusted net income, which can help you stay below the respective £100,000 and £60,000 thresholds where these benefits are withdrawn).

Table 7 shows how the £2,000 cap may affect employees and employers.

For example, someone who has a base salary of £75,000 and sacrifices 5% (£3,750) in exchange for an employer pension contribution will currently be saving £75 national insurance (£3,750 x 2%) and their employer will be saving £563 (£3,750 x 15%).

When the £2,000 cap comes into force, they will pay an extra £35 national insurance (£3,750 – £2,000 = £1,750 x 2% = £35) and their employer will pay an additional £263 (£1,750 x 15% = £263).

Clearly, most of the additional national insurance burden will fall on employers who do not pass on their national insurance savings to their employees (in the form of higher pension contributions).

Employees who do currently benefit from their employers' national insurance savings could see the amount going into their pensions reduced.

Of course, some employers may simply cease to offer a salary sacrifice pension arrangement, which would remove the potential national insurance savings altogether, making the exemption for the first £2,000 irrelevant.

Regular Employer Pension Contributions

There were rumours circulating before the November 2025 Budget that employer's national insurance could become payable on ALL employer pension contributions, not just on sacrificed salaries.

Thankfully, the £2,000 cap will not apply to pension contributions made outside a salary sacrifice arrangement. It will not apply to pension contributions made by the employer out of its own funds. Only contributions made out of earnings that have been given up by the employee will be affected.

Thus there will continue to be no national insurance payable on regular employer pension contributions.

This is also good news for small company owners who get their companies to make pension contributions as an alternative to paying themselves salary or dividend income (see Chapter 26).

Based on the information available at present, the £2,000 cap is unlikely to apply where the director does not have an employment contract which gives them a right to a higher salary that is subsequently given up. Because there is no sacrifice of existing contractual earnings, the company pension contribution should be treated as a regular employer contribution, exempt from national insurance.

Tax Avoidance Clampdown?

It remains to be seen how the Government will clamp down on those who take steps to replicate the national insurance benefits of salary sacrifice pensions by other means.

The £2,000 cap applies to amounts that would otherwise have been paid as salary. Ordinary (non-salary sacrificed) employer contributions will remain exempt from national insurance.

This raises the question whether employers could try to replicate the national insurance benefits of existing salary sacrifice arrangements by, for example, limiting future pay increases and instead only offering employees higher employer pension contributions?

The Office for Budget Responsibility (OBR) has also pointed out that: *"It would also be possible to formally replicate salary sacrifice through an agreement to reduce wages and increase employer pension contributions."* However, the OBR also points out that: *"this behaviour would be constrained by the Operational Remuneration Agreement (OPRA) rules and employment law meaning that such reductions would need to be agreed with the entire workforce"*.

The OPRA rules are designed to prevent employees choosing between cash salary and most non-cash benefits (but not pensions at present) to reduce tax.

We will have to wait and see what anti-avoidance measures HMRC introduces to prevent employers offering bigger pension contributions to employees outside of traditional salary sacrifice arrangements.

It also remains to be seen whether measures will be introduced to prevent employers and employees from making unusually large pensions contributions before 6th April 2029, to take advantage of the current national insurance savings.

Part 6

Company Directors

Chapter 25

Introduction

Company directors, just like regular employees, can contribute up to 100% of their 'relevant UK earnings' to a pension and receive full tax relief ...but typically not more than £60,000 per year (the annual allowance).

Your relevant UK earnings will include your:

- Salary and any bonus
- Taxable benefits in kind

For example, a company director with a salary of £20,000 can make a cash contribution of up to £16,000. The taxman will top this up with £4,000 of basic-rate tax relief for a gross pension contribution of £20,000.

A company director whose only income is a salary of £80,000 can make a cash contribution of up to £48,000. The taxman will top this up with £12,000 of basic-rate tax relief for a gross pension contribution of £60,000. He can make an additional pension contribution of £20,000 gross if he has unused annual allowance from any of the previous three tax years.

(Of course, as we saw in Chapter 4, the director may not want to make such a large contribution in practice because he would not receive higher-rate tax relief on the whole contribution.)

Company Pension Contributions

As a company owner you can also get your company (your employer) to make pension contributions on your behalf. Company pension contributions are always paid *gross* (there is no top up from the taxman) but the company will normally enjoy corporation tax relief on the payment.

Companies currently pay between 19% and 26.5% corporation tax. Thus a company pension contribution of £10,000 will enjoy between £1,900 and £2,650 of corporation tax relief.

Pension contributions made by employers are not restricted by the level of the employee's earnings. Thus a company pension contribution can be bigger than the director's earnings.

However, there are other restrictions on company pension contributions:

- Firstly, total pension contributions by you and your company must not exceed the £60,000 annual allowance, although any unused allowance from the previous three tax years can be carried forward and used to cover contributions made by both you and the company. (High income earners may be subject to a lower annual allowance – see Chapter 21.)

- Secondly, the company may be denied corporation tax relief on any pension contributions made on behalf of directors, if the taxman views them as 'excessive'. We'll return to this point later.

In this part of the guide we explain why pension contributions are an attractive alternative to dividends.

We also answer the important question asked by many company owners: "Who should make the pension contributions: me or the company?"

However, before doing that it's important to explain how company owners often structure their pay to reduce income tax and national insurance.

Chapter 26

Salary or Dividend?

Most small company owners are both directors and shareholders. This means they can withdraw both salaries and dividends from their companies. Salaries are subject to income tax and national insurance, dividends are subject to income tax only.

Taking a big salary is usually very expensive because of the national insurance cost. Up to 8% national insurance will have to be paid by the company owner personally and an extra 15% may have to be paid by the company (unless it is covered by the £10,500 employment allowance).

But extracting all the profits as dividends is not the best solution either for most small company owners because this means subjecting all of the company's profits to corporation tax (dividends are paid out of after-tax profits).

The optimal solution in many cases is to take a small salary that is tax deductible in the company's hands and mostly free from national insurance in the hands of the director.

"Optimal" Salaries for 2026/27

For many company owners taking a salary of £12,570 is optimal for the current tax year (2026/27).

There won't be any employee's national insurance and, providing the company owner has no other income, the salary will also be income tax free.

Some *employer's* national insurance may be payable but the corporation tax relief on the extra payment usually outweighs the national insurance cost.

A salary of £12,570 will not be optimal for everyone, however. A higher or lower salary may be more tax efficient for some directors.

For a complete discussion of this topic see the Taxcafe guide *Salary versus Dividends*.

What Has This Got to Do with Pensions?

If you get your company to pay you a small salary because it is tax efficient to do so, you can only make a small pension contribution personally. This is because, to enjoy tax relief, your pension contributions cannot exceed your earnings. However, your *company* can make pension contributions on your behalf and these will not be restricted by your small salary.

How Dividends Are Taxed

Once they've paid themselves a small salary, many company owners take the rest of their income as dividends.

Dividends are subject to income tax but not national insurance. The income tax rates on dividends are lower than those applying to salaries because dividends are paid out of a company's *after-tax* profits: the money has already been taxed in the company's hands, whereas salaries are a tax deductible expense.

From 6th April 2026 most income tax rates on dividend income have been increased by 2%.

For those receiving dividends in excess of the £500 dividend allowance, the following tax rates apply:

	2025/26	**2026/27 Onwards**
Basic rate taxpayers	8.75%	10.75%
Higher rate taxpayers	33.75%	35.75%
Additional rate taxpayers	39.35%	39.35%

Note the additional rate has NOT been increased.

Because income paid as dividends is taxed twice (first in the hands of the company and second in the hands of the shareholder) it's easy to lose sight of how much tax is being paid overall. As a company owner you are possibly just as concerned about your company's tax bill as your own, so it's worth showing the overall combined tax rates on dividend income.

Before we do that it's first worth briefly outlining how much corporation tax companies pay on their profits.

How Companies Are Taxed

On 1st April 2023 the main rate of corporation tax increased from 19% to 25%. Companies now pay tax as follows:

- **Profits £50,000 or less** – Company pays 19% tax on all of its profits
- **Profits between £50,000 and £250,000** – Company pays 19% tax on the first £50,000 and 26.5% on the remainder
- **Profits greater than £250,000** – Company pays 25% tax on all of its profits

Combined Tax Rates on Dividend Income

For a company paying 19% corporation tax on all of its profits the combined tax rates (corporation tax and income tax) on dividend income are as follows:

	Combined Tax Rate
Basic-rate taxpayers	28%
Higher-rate taxpayers	48%
Additional-rate taxpayers	51%

For example, if the company has £1,000 of profit on which it has paid £190 corporation tax, this leaves £810 to pay as dividends. A higher-rate taxpayer will pay £290 tax on this income (£810 x 35.75%), so the total tax on the £1,000 profit is £480, i.e. 48%.

For a company with profits between £50,000 and £250,000 the combined marginal tax rates are as follows:

	Combined Marginal Tax Rate
Basic rate taxpayers	34%
Higher rate taxpayers	53%
Additional rate taxpayers	55%

The above tax rates are a fair bit higher than the income tax rates that apply to most types of income.

This is supposed to level the playing field between company owners (who often pay little or no national insurance because they take most of their income as dividends) and self-employed business owners and regular employees, who pay national insurance on most of their earnings.

Company owners are also an easy target for politicians.

From a tax planning perspective, company owners may be better off paying themselves other types income that are taxed at a lower overall rate in preference to dividends, where possible.

Examples include interest income (if you have lent money to your company) and rental income (if your company occupies premises that you own personally).

The income tax rates payable on these types of income are increasing by 2% on 6th April 2027, which means basic-rate taxpayers will pay 22%, higher-rate taxpayers 42% and additional-rate taxpayers 47%. However, these rates are still lower than the combined tax rates applying to dividend income.

As a result of the 2023 corporation tax increase many companies are now enjoying more corporation tax relief on pension contributions they make for their directors and employees (up to 26.5%), as we shall see in the next chapter.

A Final Word on Company Owners and their Pay

Finally, please note that I am not recommending that company owners structure their pay in the way described in this chapter. You should always speak to an accountant about your own optimal pay structure.

Chapter 27

Pension Contributions: Better than Dividends?

Thanks to the 2023 increase in corporation tax many companies are enjoying more tax relief on any pension contributions they make for their directors and employees.

Previously companies enjoyed at most 19% tax relief but this has risen to 26.5% for companies with profits between £50,000 and £250,000 and 25% for companies with profits over £250,000.

A company with profits of £100,000 would previously have saved £1,900 corporation tax by making a pension contribution of £10,000. With a marginal tax rate of 26.5% it will now save £2,650.

Coupled with the latest increase in dividend tax rates, many company owners may find it even more appealing to get their companies to make pension contributions, instead of paying themselves additional dividend income.

There are several reasons why pension contributions are an attractive alternative to dividends:

- Like salaries, company pension contributions enjoy corporation tax relief. They're a tax deductible business expense.

- Unlike salaries, there is no national insurance on the income you eventually withdraw from your pension.

- Up to 25% of your pension savings can be taken as a tax-free lump sum (capped at £268,275 for most people).

- Pension income is taxed at the "regular" income tax rates, typically 20% or 40%. By contrast, the combined tax rate (corporation tax and income tax) on dividend income has risen to *at least* 28% for basic-rate taxpayers and 48% for higher-rate taxpayers.

- When you start withdrawing money from your pension, you could find yourself in a lower tax bracket than you are now (many retirees are basic-rate taxpayers).

Putting all this together, it's possible that you could ultimately pay income tax on your pension withdrawals at an effective rate of just 15%.

By contrast, you may face a combined tax rate that is possibly two to three times higher if the same money is paid out as dividend income.

There is, of course, a major drawback with pensions: your money is locked away until you are 55 (rising to 57 in 2028). Nevertheless, when you do reach the minimum retirement age you can make unlimited withdrawals.

Another drawback with pensions is you are potentially exposed to any future increase in income tax rates. Essentially your savings are at the mercy of future governments.

Having said this, we do believe that pension contributions are still worth making in many cases.

Example – Higher-rate Taxpayer

Lesleyanne is a company owner and a higher rate taxpayer (i.e. her taxable income is more than £50,270).

Let's say she is trying to choose between taking an additional £1,000 of the company's profit as a dividend and getting the company to invest £1,000 in her self-invested personal pension (SIPP).

Let's also say her company has a marginal corporation tax rate of 26.5% (as will often be the case). Hence, with a dividend the company will first pay corporation tax of £265, leaving £735 to distribute. Lesleyanne will then pay income tax at 35.75%: £263. The total combined tax rate on the dividend is 53%.

By contrast, a company pension contribution will enjoy corporation tax relief, so the whole £1,000 will go straight into Lesleyanne's SIPP. Ignoring investment growth (it doesn't affect the outcome), when she eventually withdraws the money from her pension, the first £250 will be tax free and the remaining £750 will be subject to income tax.

If Lesleyanne is a basic rate taxpayer when she retires in the future, she will pay 20% income tax (£150), leaving her with £850 overall. Thus, her effective overall tax rate will be 15%.

If Lesleyanne is a higher rate taxpayer when she retires (for example, if she ends up with a significant amount of rental income from buy-to-let properties) she will effectively pay 40% tax on her taxable pension income (£300), leaving her with £700 overall. Thus, the effective tax rate on her pension withdrawals will be 30%.

In summary, Lesleyanne's choice is between paying tax at 53% on her additional dividend income and paying tax at 15% or possibly 30% on her pension withdrawals.

What this example shows is that, for company owners who have not already built up significant pension savings, a company pension contribution is an extremely attractive alternative to additional dividend income.

Of course, one must never lose sight of the fact that your pension savings are placed in a locked box until you are at least 55. So a company pension contribution is only an attractive alternative to a dividend if you have already withdrawn enough money from your company to cover your living costs.

In the above example we assumed that the company has a marginal tax rate of 26.5%. If its profits are no greater than £50,000 the combined tax rate on Lesleyanne's additional dividend income will be 48% and if its profits are greater than £250,000 the combined tax rate will be 52% – compared with 15% or possibly 30% on her pension withdrawals.

Are company pension contributions attractive if you're a basic-rate taxpayer (taxable income less than £50,270)? Let's find out:

Example – Basic-rate Taxpayer

Poppy is a company owner and a basic-rate taxpayer.

She too is trying to choose between taking £1,000 of the company's profit as a dividend and a £1,000 company pension contribution.

Let's assume the company's profits do not exceed £50,000 which means it will pay corporation tax at 19%. With a dividend the company will first pay corporation tax of £190, leaving £810 to distribute. Poppy will then pay income tax at 10.75%: £87. The total combined tax rate on the dividend is 28%.

If the company has profits in the £50,000-£250,000 bracket it will face a marginal corporation tax rate of 26.5% which means it will pay £265 tax and the total combined tax rate on the dividend will be 34%.

Alternatively, with a company pension contribution the whole £1,000 will go straight into Poppy's SIPP. As with Lesleyanne, the effective tax rate on her pension withdrawals will be either 15% if she is a basic-rate taxpayer when she retires or 30% if she is a higher-rate taxpayer.

In summary, Poppy's choice is between paying tax at between 28% or 34% on her additional dividend income and paying tax at 15% or possibly 30% on her future pension withdrawals.

What this example shows is that, if you are currently a basic-rate taxpayer, a company pension contribution is a reasonably attractive alternative to additional dividend income.

However, pension contributions will not be very attractive if you end up wealthier in retirement and become a higher-rate taxpayer. This could happen if, for example, you inherit or accumulate a significant amount of assets and the income takes you over the higher-rate threshold before you start withdrawing money from your pension.

Chapter 28

Pension Contributions: You or the Company?

In the previous chapter we saw that company pension contributions can be an attractive alternative to dividends. However, company directors can also make pension contributions personally, so a key question is: *"Who should make the contributions: the director or the company?"*

Company Owner Pension Contributions

When you make pension contributions *personally* (as opposed to getting your company to make them) the taxman will top up your savings by paying cash directly into your pension. For every £80 you invest the taxman will put in an extra £20.

Why £20? Your contributions are treated as having been paid out of income that has already been taxed at 20%, the basic rate of income tax.

The company that manages your pension plan – usually an insurance company or SIPP provider – will claim this money for you from the taxman and credit it to your account.

So whatever contribution you make personally, divide it by 0.80 and you'll get the total amount that is invested in your pension pot (your gross pension contribution).

Example
Peter is a company owner who takes most of his income as dividends. He invests £800 in a self-invested personal pension (SIPP). The taxman will top up his pension with £200 of basic-rate tax relief which means he'll have £1,000 in his pension pot: £800/0.80 = £1,000.

If Peter is a higher-rate taxpayer he can also claim higher-rate tax relief when he completes his tax return. This is given by increasing his basic-rate band by the amount of his gross pension contribution.

Example continued

Peter's gross pension contribution is £1,000 so his basic-rate band will be increased by £1,000. This means £1,000 of his dividend income will be taxed at 10.75% instead of 35.75%, i.e. a 25% saving. Thus, Peter's higher-rate tax relief is: £1,000 x 25% = £250.

In total Peter will enjoy £450 of tax relief (£200 basic-rate relief plus £250 higher-rate tax relief). Peter's total tax relief is 45% of his £1,000 gross pension contribution.

Company Directors with Small Salaries

To obtain tax relief on your pension contributions they have to stay within certain limits:

- **Earnings.** Contributions made by you *personally* must not exceed your 'relevant UK earnings'. Earnings include your salary, bonus and taxable benefits in kind but do NOT include your dividends. (Note, almost everyone can make a gross contribution of £3,600, regardless of income.)

- **The £60,000 Annual Allowance.** Total pension contributions by you and your company must not exceed £60,000 per year, although it is possible to carry forward any unused annual allowance from the three previous tax years. The annual allowance is reduced if your 'adjusted income' exceeds £260,000 (see Chapter 21).

For a company director taking a salary of £12,570 (see Chapter 26) the maximum gross pension contribution is £12,570. The director would personally invest £10,056 (£12,570 x 80%) and the taxman will top this up with £2,514 of basic-rate tax relief for a total gross contribution of £12,570.

If the director wants to make bigger pension contributions personally they will have to pay themselves a bigger salary.

However, this may not be an attractive option because a bigger salary may be subject to employer's national insurance at 15% or employee's national insurance at 8%, or both.

Company Pension Contributions

As a company owner, you can also get your company (your employer) to make pension contributions on your behalf. Company pension contributions are always paid *gross* (there is no top up from the taxman), but the company will normally enjoy corporation tax relief on the payment. For example, a company with a marginal corporation tax rate of 26.5% can make a pension contribution of £10,000 and enjoy £2,650 of tax relief.

You do not need a dedicated company pension scheme to make company pension contributions. Most firms that offer SIPPs allow your company to pay directly into your pension (these plans may not be qualifying schemes for auto-enrolment purposes, however).

Prior to the November 2025 Budget there were rumours the Government would introduce national insurance on employers' pension contributions. Thankfully no such change was announced. Companies can continue to make pension contributions exempt from employer's national insurance. Only salary sacrifice pension contributions will be capped: from April 2029.

How much can your company contribute? Unlike the contributions you make personally, the company's contributions are NOT restricted by the size of your salary. In other words, the company can make a pension contribution that is bigger than your salary. However, there are other restrictions:

- Total pension contributions by you and your company must not exceed the annual allowance (typically £60,000) although you can carry forward unused allowance from the previous three tax years.

- The company may be denied corporation tax relief on any pension contributions made on behalf of directors, if the taxman views them as 'excessive'.

Corporation Tax Relief on Pension Contributions

Unlike the pension contributions that you make personally, tax relief for company pension contributions is not automatic. Company contributions will only be a tax deductible expense for corporation tax purposes if they are incurred wholly and exclusively for the purposes of the business. There is a danger that HMRC will deny corporation tax relief for 'excessive' pension contributions. In practice this is relatively rare.

To determine whether company contributions qualify for corporation tax relief, HMRC will look at the total remuneration package of the director. The total package (including salary, pension contributions and other benefits) must not be excessive relative to the work carried out and his or her responsibilities.

Relevant factors may include:

- The number of hours you work, your experience and your level of responsibility in the company
- The pay of unconnected employees in your company and other companies who perform duties of similar value
- The pay required to recruit someone to take over your duties
- The company's financial performance

Extra care may be necessary in the event of a large one-off company pension contribution.

It may be sensible to document the commercial justification (for example, strong recent financial performance of the company) in the minutes of a directors' board meeting and hold a shareholders' meeting to approve the contribution.

In some cases, when a company is making pension contributions on behalf of all employees (including directors) of more than £500,000 in total, it may be necessary to spread tax relief for the excess over a number of years. These spreading rules will obviously not affect most small companies.

Although the risk that your company will be denied corporation tax relief may be small, it is important to stress that, when it comes to company pension contributions, unlike contributions made by individuals, there is no cast-iron guarantee that the company will enjoy tax relief.

That's why we would recommend speaking to a tax adviser before your company starts making significant contributions.

Pension Contributions: You or the Company?

Using a couple of case studies we will now compare company pension contributions with pension contributions made personally by company owners to see which is most tax efficient.

Case Study 1: Basic-rate Taxpayer, 19% Corporation Tax

Eva owns Cassidy Ltd. She is a basic-rate taxpayer and pays herself a salary of £12,570 this year and takes the rest of her income as dividends.

She also decides to use £1,000 of the company's pre-tax profit to fund a pension contribution. If Cassidy Ltd makes the contribution it can pay £1,000 directly into Eva's SIPP and the amount will be a tax deductible expense.

Alternatively Eva can pay herself a dividend to fund a pension contribution she makes personally. We'll assume the company pays 19% corporation tax on the £1,000 profit, leaving Eva with £810 to take as dividend income.

Eva will have to pay 10.75% tax on her £810 dividend, leaving her with £723 to invest in her SIPP. The taxman will add £181 of basic-rate tax relief, leaving her with £904 in her pension.

In summary, Eva ends up with almost 11% more money in her pension if the *company* makes the contributions.

In this case a company pension contribution is clearly more tax efficient than a contribution made personally by the director.

Other Important Points

If Eva wants more than £12,570 invested in her pension, making the contribution personally will be even more expensive.

She would have to pay herself a bigger salary, so that she has more "earnings" and this could result in a significant amount of national insurance becoming payable. The additional salary will typically attract 8% employee's national insurance and 15% employer's national insurance, unless the company has spare employment allowance.

Case Study 2: Higher Rate Taxpayer, 26.5% Corporation Tax

This time we'll assume Eva is a *higher rate taxpayer* and again wants to make a £1,000 pension contribution.

If Cassidy Ltd makes the contribution, it can pay £1,000 directly into Eva's SIPP. Alternatively, Eva can pay herself an extra dividend. Assuming the company pays 26.5% corporation tax on the £1,000 profit, Eva will be left with £735 to take as dividend income.

Thus Eva may have to contribute up to £65 out of her own pocket to invest £800 in her SIPP. The taxman will add £200 basic rate tax relief, resulting in the same gross pension contribution of £1,000.

However, that's not the end of the matter. Eva still has to pay income tax on the additional dividend.

With a gross pension contribution of £1,000, Eva's basic rate band will be increased by £1,000. This means the extra dividend of £735 will be taxed at just 10.75%, not 35.75%, so the tax is £79.

Furthermore, an additional £265 of her other dividend income will also be taxed at 10.75% instead of 35.75%, saving her £66.

All in all, a £1,000 pension contribution made by the director is £78 more expensive than a contribution made by the company:

£79 income tax + £65 (cash added) – £66 extra relief = £78

A company pension contribution is again more tax efficient than a contribution made personally by the director, producing an overall saving of 7.8%.

Other Important Points

If Eva wants to enjoy full higher rate tax relief on a gross personal contribution of £12,570 (i.e. equal to her salary), she must have at least £12,570 of dividend income above the higher rate threshold (total income of at least £62,840 in 2026/27).

And if Eva wants to make a pension contribution bigger than £12,570 personally, she will have to take a bigger salary and this may result in a significant amount of national insurance becoming payable.

Additional-rate Taxpayers

Those who have income over £125,140 face a marginal income tax rate of 39.35% on their dividend income.

These individuals will also generally end up better off by getting their companies to make pension contributions, instead of funding them personally out of additional dividend income.

However, probably the most important point to make here is that a high earning company owner who takes a salary of £12,570 (see Chapter 26) can only make a gross pension contribution of £12,570 personally. That is a relatively small pension contribution for someone with income of, say £150,000 or £200,000.

Those company owners who want to put more money into their pensions personally would have to pay themselves more salary. But this is usually not tax efficient because a significant amount of national insurance may be payable on the additional salary income.

In fact, as we point out in the Taxcafe guide *Salary versus Dividends*, a salary *lower* than £12,570 may sometimes be 'optimal' for high income earners, possibly no more than the £6,708 lower earnings limit. Such a salary would be just big enough to keep building your state pension entitlement. A pension contribution of £6,708 would almost certainly be too small for any high income earner who is still actively saving for retirement.

For this reason a company pension contribution will usually be the best route for those high earners who want to make contributions that are big enough to build a respectable pension pot.

When Personal Contributions Are Attractive

Making pension contributions personally is still worth considering in some situations, for example when your income accidentally goes over one of the key tax thresholds.

Take the example of a director who always tries to keep his taxable income below the £50,270 higher-rate threshold but estimates that he will have, say, £55,000 this year. If he makes a gross pension contribution of £4,730 personally this will prevent any of his dividend income being taxed at the 35.75% higher rate.

Lifetime ISA versus Company Pension Contributions

In Chapter 15 we examined the Lifetime ISA. Like pensions they attract a top up from the Government but, unlike pensions, ALL the money you take out will be tax free.

Let's say a company owner who is a basic rate taxpayer is trying to decide between a £1,000 company pension contribution and using a dividend to fund a Lifetime ISA contribution.

A £1,000 pension contribution will attract corporation tax relief so the whole £1,000 will go directly into the company owner's pension.

If the same money is used to pay a dividend to fund a Lifetime ISA contribution, and assuming the company pays 19% corporation tax, £810 will be left to pay out. After paying 10.75% income tax, the company owner will be left with £723 to invest in a Lifetime ISA. Adding the Government bonus, the company owner will end up with £904 in the Lifetime ISA.

When the company owner reaches age 60, all withdrawals from the Lifetime ISA will be tax free, whereas only 25% of the money withdrawn from the pension will be tax free (although they can get it slightly earlier). The rest will possibly be taxed at just 20% if they are a basic rate taxpayer in retirement.

If we ignore investment growth to keep the example simple (it doesn't affect the outcome), with a Lifetime ISA the company owner will end up with £904; with a pension they will end up with just £850 after tax.

Thus, if you're a basic rate taxpayer, you could end up with 6.3% more money from a Lifetime ISA.

And, if you're a higher rate taxpayer when you retire, you could end up with 29% more money from a Lifetime ISA.

On the other hand, if your company is paying corporation tax at more than 19%, the advantage of a Lifetime ISA will be reduced, or could even be eliminated.

For example, at the highest marginal corporation tax rate of 26.5%, £1,000 of pre-tax profit will only fund a dividend of £735. After income tax at 10.75%, a basic rate taxpayer will be left with £656. If they put that in a Lifetime ISA, the Government will add £164 for a total investment of £820. In the end, if they're a basic rate taxpayer when they retire, a company pension contribution could have left them with £850, i.e. £30 more.

The difference is only marginal, however, and it's important to remember, if you're a higher rate taxpayer when you draw your pension, you might end up with only £700 after tax.

So, basic rate taxpayers who own a company making profits between £50,000 and £250,000 face a choice between a certain £820 from a Lifetime ISA, or a possible £850 from a pension that might, in fact, only be £700.

Pension vs Lifetime ISA: Higher Rate Taxpayers

What about higher rate taxpayers? Once again, a £1,000 pension contribution will attract corporation tax relief, so the whole £1,000 will go directly into the company owner's pension.

If the same money is used to pay a dividend to fund a Lifetime ISA contribution, the amount received by the director will vary depending on the company's marginal corporation tax rate. If we assume it's 26.5%, the amount left to pay a dividend will be £735. After paying 35.75% income tax, the company owner will be left with £472 to invest in their Lifetime ISA. Adding the Government bonus, the company owner will end up with £590 in their Lifetime ISA.

When the company owner reaches age 60, all withdrawals from the Lifetime ISA will be tax free, whereas only 25% of the money withdrawn from the pension will be tax free. The rest could be taxed at just 20% if they are a basic-rate taxpayer at that point.

Ignoring investment growth again, with a Lifetime ISA the company owner will end up with £590, with a pension they will end up with £850 after tax.

Thus, your retirement income could be up to 44% higher with a pension.

If the company owner is a higher rate taxpayer when they retire (e.g. if they have a lot of income from other sources, such as rental property) they will end up with £700 from a pension, compared with £590 from a Lifetime ISA. So, again, a company pension contribution will generally be better.

It's also important to remember you can only invest £4,000 per year in a Lifetime ISA (with an additional £1,000 bonus from the Government), compared with the maximum gross pension contribution of £60,000 per year.

Furthermore, you can only open a Lifetime ISA if you're under 40, and it's only possible to make contributions up to age 50.

Finally, as mentioned in Chapter 14, the future of the Lifetime ISA as a retirement saving vehicle is somewhat in doubt at the time of writing, following an announcement in the November 2025 Budget.

Summary

- A company owner who takes a salary of, say, £12,570 is restricted to making a gross pension contribution of just £12,570 *personally*.

- As a company owner you can get your company to make pension contributions on your behalf. Company pension contributions are typically more tax efficient than contributions made personally by directors.

- Tax relief for company pension contributions is not automatic – tax relief could be denied if the contributions are viewed as excessive, although this is rare in practice.

- A company pension contribution is usually more tax efficient than a Lifetime ISA investment if you are a higher-rate taxpayer when you make the investment.

Chapter 29

Taking a Loan from Your Small Self-Administered Scheme (SSAS)

In Chapter 32 we will see how your pension savings can be used to buy commercial property.

This isn't the only way your pension savings can be used to help your business.

Your pension pot can also be used to make a loan to your company.

To do this you will probably have to set up a "small self-administered scheme" (SSAS).

A SSAS is a type of occupational pension scheme, typically established by the owner-managers of a small company (the "sponsoring employer").

SSAS Basics

Although a self-invested personal pension (SIPP) can be used to buy commercial property, a SIPP cannot be used to make a loan to your company.

In theory all pension schemes can make loans to *third parties* but loans to members (or those connected to members) are generally not allowed.

Loans to the sponsoring employers of occupational pension schemes are an exception. A SSAS is an occupational scheme and can therefore lend money to the company that sets it up.

A loan cannot be made to the individual members of the pension scheme or their close relatives or other companies controlled by the members (unless those companies are sponsoring employers of the pension scheme too).

A pension loan can be used for a variety of reasons, for example to buy equipment or stock for the business. However, it cannot be used to a keep a failing company afloat or to directly benefit the members.

A SSAS will typically have no more than 11 members and each member will be a "member trustee" with power over how the money is invested. This exempts the SSAS from certain aspects of the pensions legislation, giving it more flexibility.

Small self-administered schemes are offered by a number of specialist pension companies. They provide all the documentation to establish the SSAS, register it with HMRC, act as the "professional trustee" and manage the day-to-day administration.

Setting up and running a SSAS is much more expensive than a conventional SIPP so there's no point using one unless you need the extra flexibility.

For example, one pension company I looked at briefly is charging £1,890 to set up a SSAS and an annual administration fee of £2,260. Further fees are then payable to arrange and administer a loan from the pension scheme.

With a SSAS there may also be quite a few additional one-off and ongoing charges. Some of these fees are fixed, others are levied on a time cost basis (something which always makes me nervous).

Further fees may also be incurred when taking out a loan from the pension scheme, for example obtaining a professional valuation for the assets used as security.

Costs vary from pension company to pension company. You can find out what's on offer by simply doing internet searches using phrases that include "SSAS".

Fees can be paid by the sponsoring company rather than the pension scheme.

Pension Loans – The Rules

Borrowing money from your pension may be more attractive than borrowing from a bank or other conventional lender.

However, it's important to note that your pension scheme cannot give your company a soft loan with no interest payable and flexible repayment terms.

There are several rules that have to be obeyed to avoid so-called "unauthorised payment" tax charges:

Interest Rate

The minimum interest rate that must be charged is set out in HMRC's Prescribed Interest Rates for Authorised Employer Loans.

The interest rate must be *at least* 1% higher than the average of the base lending rates of six big UK banks: Bank of Scotland, Barclays, HSBC, Lloyds, Natwest and RBS.

The average rate is rounded up to the nearest 0.25%.

The current minimum interest rate that must be used can be found on HMRC's website under "Interest charged on underpaid quarterly instalment payments":

https://tinyurl.com/emploanrates

At the time of writing the current minimum interest rate is 6.25%.

Higher interest rates can be charged and some of the case studies on the pension companies' websites use interest rates closer to 10%.

The point is that, even if a high rate of interest is charged, at least "it's all kept in the family": the interest payments go from *your* company to *your* pension scheme.

The interest payments will be a tax deductible business expense for the company and tax-free income for the pension scheme (because pension schemes don't pay tax on their investment income).

Security

The loan has to be secured by means of a first charge over assets with a value equal to the loan plus all the interest payable on the loan.

The company may be prevented from taking a pension loan if it already has a "floating charge" over its assets.

Some pension administrators insist that the security must be in the form of land or bricks and mortar property.

Other pension companies accept security in the form of intellectual property owned by the company (for example its trademark, customer database etc).

The asset does not have to be owned by the company.

Whatever asset is used it will have to be independently valued, which will result in additional professional fees being incurred.

Using residential property as security for the loan has to be handled extremely carefully. This is because pension schemes are prohibited from owning residential property in most circumstances. The loan has to be structured in such a way that, if the pension scheme has to foreclose, it will not take ownership of any residential property used as security. This would result in hefty unauthorised payment tax charges.

Some pension companies will not allow residential property to be used as security.

Maximum Loan

The loan must not exceed 50% of the net asset value of the pension scheme. So you cannot lend all your pension savings to your company.

Any excess above 50% is treated as an unauthorised payment.

This calculation is performed when the loan is taken out. It doesn't matter if the pension scheme's assets fall in value thereafter.

Length of Loan

The maximum term of the loan is five years. The loan can be rolled over once for another five years in certain circumstances if the company is in genuine financial difficulty.

Repaying the Loan

The loan must be repaid in equal instalments of capital and interest, with at least one payment per year.

If payments fall short an unauthorised payment is deemed to have been made by the pension scheme.

The trustees must take any action necessary to ensure that the loan is repaid, even if this means forcing the company into liquidation.

Unauthorised Payments

If the above rules are broken this could result in an unauthorised payment from the pension scheme.

Unauthorised payments are subject to prohibitive tax charges:

- Unauthorised payment charge – 40% payable by the company
- Scheme sanction charge – 15% payable by the pension scheme administrator (40% if the unauthorised payment charge has not been paid)
- Unauthorised payment surcharge – 15% payable by the company if the unauthorised payments exceed 25% of the value of the pension scheme.

Are Pension Loans a Good Idea?

So is it a good idea to get your company to borrow money from your pension?

One danger is you could end up putting most of your eggs into one basket. If your business goes belly up, you could end up losing a big chunk of your retirement savings as well.

For the same reason it could be argued that business owners should never borrow against their homes.

These three major assets – your business, your pension and your home – should, arguably, be kept completely separate.

This may be a bit unrealistic in practice, however. Borrowing money from a bank is often just as risky for the company owners themselves because banks will usually insist on personal guarantees, typically putting the family home at risk.

In any case why shouldn't an experienced business owner tap their pension pot for a loan if the money will be invested prudently in their business?

Although borrowing from your pension may be acceptable in certain circumstances, I think it would be bordering on insanity to transfer out of a final salary scheme to a SSAS for this purpose.

Are Pension Loans Tax Efficient?

Earlier it was mentioned that, if your company borrows money from your pension scheme, the interest payments will be a tax deductible business expense for the company and tax-free income for the pension scheme.

Does this mean that borrowing money from your pension is tax efficient? Not really. If your company borrowed money from a bank the interest payments would also be tax deductible expense. And the money left in your pension scheme could be invested somewhere else and the investment returns would also be tax free.

However, borrowing from your pension could be less costly overall.

Example – Borrowing from Pension

Jacinda's company, Kiwi Holidays Ltd, needs £100,000 to buy some new equipment.

Jacinda has £200,000 of pension savings, recently transferred into a SSAS.

Let's say Kiwi Holidays borrows £100,000 from the pension scheme and pays 7% interest. For simplicity's sake we will assume the loan is for just one year. The company uses its sales income to repay the loan.

One year later, after the loan is repaid, Jacinda's pension pot will have an additional £7,000 of tax-free interest.

Jacinda's company will have paid out £7,000 interest, with corporation tax relief available on the full amount.

The company will also have paid out £100,000 repaying the initial loan amount but will have £100,000 more equipment.

Example – Borrowing from a Bank

The facts are exactly the same except this time Jacinda's company borrows from a bank instead of her pension.

Let's say Kiwi Holidays pays 7% interest on the bank loan and her pension savings enjoy a return of 7% when invested elsewhere.

One year later Jacinda's pension pot will have an additional £7,000 of tax-free returns, just as in the above example.

Jacinda's company will have paid out £7,000 interest, with corporation tax relief available on the full amount, just as in the above example.

And just as in the above example, the company will have paid out £100,000 repaying the initial loan amount but will have £100,000 more equipment.

In summary, from a *tax* perspective, borrowing from your pension is exactly the same as borrowing from a bank.

However, Jacinda may end up better off overall if the bank charges her company more interest than she can earn on her pension investments.

Example Revised – Borrowing from Bank

Let's say Kiwi Holidays pays 10% interest on the bank loan and her pension savings enjoy investment returns of 7%.

One year later Jacinda's pension pot will have an additional £7,000 of tax-free returns, just as in the above examples.

But Jacinda's company will have paid out £10,000 interest to the bank. Tax relief can, of course, be claimed on this interest, just as in the previous examples.

The company will also pay out £100,000 repaying the initial loan amount but will have £100,000 more equipment, just as in the above examples.

Jacinda's company ends up with £3,000 less cash by borrowing from a bank (although up to £795 of this will be recovered in additional corporation tax relief).

So it would appear that company owners are better off borrowing from their pensions if the interest rate charged by a third party lender is higher than the return that can be earned on the pension scheme's investments.

When comparing bank borrowing with pension scheme borrowing it's also important to take account of all the costs. As we saw earlier, setting up and running a SSAS, and making arrangements to take a loan, will result in a variety of fees and charges.

Borrowing from the Company Owners

A company can also borrow money from the *company owners* themselves.

The company owners can charge the company interest and, as in all the above examples, the company will be able to claim corporation tax relief on the interest payments, as long as the interest rate charged is not unreasonable.

The company owner is not obliged to charge the company interest, although this is often advisable.

The interest payments from the company will be taxable income in the hands of the company owner. However, it's possible for some company owners to receive up to £6,000 of tax-free interest income every year thanks to the personal savings allowance and starting rate band.

The personal savings allowance allows you to earn up to £1,000 of tax-free interest if you are a basic-rate taxpayer and £500 if you are a higher-rate taxpayer (nothing if you are an additional-rate taxpayer).

The starting rate band allows you to earn up to £5,000 of tax-free interest. It can only be used by company owners who have less than £5,000 of *taxable non-savings income* (typically salary income and rental income but not dividends).

The £5,000 starting rate band can usually only be fully enjoyed by company owners who take a small salary (typically no more than the £12,570 personal allowance) and have little or no rental income or other non-savings income.

It's also important to point out that both the £1,000/£500 savings allowance and £5,000 starting rate band eat up your basic-rate band. They are not stand alone allowances. The practical effect is that, if your company pays you £6,000 of tax-free interest, it's possible that £6,000 of your dividend income will be pushed over the higher-rate threshold where it will be taxed at 35.75% instead of 10.75%.

Borrowing to Lend to Your Company

If a company owner doesn't have spare savings to lend to the company they can borrow the money personally and lend it to their company.

Within certain fairly generous limits, the company owner can then claim tax relief for the interest paid to the bank against all of their taxable income (including their interest income or dividend income).

Summary

If a company owner sets up a small self-administered scheme (SSAS) they can use some of their pension savings to make a loan to their company.

This may be attractive if obtaining a conventional bank loan would be difficult or expensive.

There are costs involved when setting up and running a SSAS and arranging a loan.

There are also strict rules that have to be followed, although a reputable pension company will make sure these are all followed to the letter.

Part 7

The Self Employed & Landlords

Chapter 30

Pension Planning for the Self Employed

The number of self-employed business owners saving for retirement has fallen dramatically in recent years. Back in the 1990s around 60% were contributing to a pension. Today the figure is closer to 18%.

When HMRC uses the term 'self employed' they are referring specifically to owners of unincorporated businesses, i.e. sole traders and partnerships. Most company owners are classified as employees (see Part 6 for more on company owners).

Most of the chapters in this guide are relevant for self-employed individuals. However, there are a few additional points that need to be made.

In particular, to maximise the tax relief on your pension contributions it is important to know how much taxable income you have. Most regular employees know how much taxable income they have: all they have to do is look at their payslips.

Many company owners also know how much taxable income they earn *personally*. The *company's* profits may fluctuate from year to year but many directors know how much salary or dividend income they are going to withdraw.

The taxable income of self-employed business owners is often much harder to predict. Taxable income for these individuals is normally the pre-tax profits of the business and there could be significant swings from year to year. For example, a big order before the end of the tax year could increase taxable profits significantly. Several months of poor trading conditions could see profits fall sharply or even produce a loss for the year.

Sometimes it's not just the sales of the business that will result in big changes to taxable income. The business owner may deliberately drive down taxable profits, for example by making investments in tax-deductible equipment.

So what has all this got to do with maximising tax relief on pension contributions?

In Chapter 2 we pointed out that to enjoy any tax relief on your pension contributions you must have 'relevant UK earnings'. If your business makes a loss you won't have any earnings and the maximum pension contribution you can make is £3,600 (the 'universal pension contribution' everyone under age 75 can make).

In Chapter 4 we pointed out that to maximise your higher-rate tax relief, your gross pension contributions should not exceed the amount of income you have over the higher-rate threshold (£50,270 in most parts of the UK, £43,662 in Scotland).

In other words, someone living in England with taxable income of £60,000, who wants to maximise their higher-rate tax relief, should make a gross pension contribution of no more than £9,730 (£60,000 – £50,270).

A sole trader with bumper profits of £90,000 may wish to make a big catch-up contribution of almost £40,000 but halt contributions if taxable profits fall below the higher-rate threshold.

In Chapter 18 we discussed the pros and cons of postponing pension contributions if you are a temporary basic-rate taxpayer. During tough economic times (or if the business has a lot of tax-deductible expenses for the year) the business owner may become a basic-rate taxpayer and decide to postpone pension contributions until he or she becomes a higher-rate taxpayer in a future tax year.

Finally, in Chapter 20 we explained why self-employed business owners, who are the highest earners in households that receive child benefit, may wish to make bigger than normal pension contributions when their profits are between £60,000 and £80,000. This will help them to reduce or avoid the child benefit tax charge and enjoy higher-rate tax relief.

Calculating Pre-tax Profits

Although many sole traders may wish to vary the amount they contribute to a pension each year in order to maximise their tax relief, the problem for some is they don't know how much profit the business is making. They may only have this information after they draw up their accounts for the year. This could be many months after the tax year has ended – when it's too late to make pension contributions (you cannot make backdated pension contributions).

Example

Elliott is a sole trader with a 31st March year end.

On 5th April 2027 (the final day of the 2026/27 tax year) he makes a net cash pension contribution of £4,000. The taxman adds £1,000 of basic-rate tax relief to produce a gross pension contribution of £5,000. Elliott expects to have pre-tax profits of over £55,270 for 2026/27 and therefore expects to receive the maximum higher-rate tax relief of £1,000 (£5,000 x 20%).

Elliott's accountant finishes drawing up the accounts for the business in July 2027 and, after taking account of all of his tax-deductible expenditure, calculates that Elliott has pre-tax profits of just £52,000.

This means Elliott will only enjoy higher-rate tax relief on £1,730 of his £5,000 gross pension contribution (£52,000 minus £50,270 higher-rate threshold), saving him just £346 in higher-rate tax (£1,730 x 20%). If Elliott had known his profits would be lower than expected, he may have held onto some of his cash and made a bigger pension contribution in a future tax year when his income was higher.

The problem for Elliott is he had just five days from the end of his business accounting period to the end of the tax year to calculate his pre-tax profits and make a pension contribution that produced the maximum amount of higher-rate tax relief.

Most business owners would find this difficult if not impossible to do and very few accountants would work to such a tight deadline.

Some business owners have a 5th of April year end and therefore no time at all to accurately calculate their pre-tax profits.

Uncertainty about the level of pre-tax profits is less of a problem for business owners who are confident their profits will significantly exceed the higher-rate threshold, especially if their pension contributions are quite modest (for example, someone who reckons pre-tax profits will be £80,000 and wants to make an £8,000 pension contribution).

Uncertainty about the level of pre-tax profits could be a problem for high earners who are making big catch-up pension contributions and want higher-rate tax relief on the whole amount (for example, someone who expects roughly £90,000 of pre-tax profit and wants to make a £40,000 pension contribution).

Changing the Accounting Year End

One way to overcome this problem in the past was to change the accounting year end of the business to a date other than the tax year. Unfortunately, the rules have changed in a way that now makes this approach not just ineffective, but even worse than having 31st March or 5th April for your accounting date.

This is because, from 2024/25 onwards, self-employed people must be taxed on a *tax year* basis. Note, if your business has a 31st March year end it can keep this date for tax purposes because this is viewed as close enough to the end of the tax year.

In fact, you can use any accounting date you like, but if it isn't between 31st March and 5th April, you will have to pro rata your results to fit the tax year. For example, if you draw up accounts to 31st December each year, your taxable profits for 2026/27 will be made up of 9/12ths of your profit for the year ending 31st December 2026 plus 3/12ths of your profit for the year ending 31st December 2027. So, you're not going to know your taxable profit for 2026/27 until sometime in 2028.

As a result of these changes many self-employed individuals will find it more difficult to work out their relevant UK earnings for pension contributions. Those serious about maximising the tax relief on their contributions may have to make an estimate of their profits before the end of the tax year.

For example, if you adopt a 31st March accounting date then, in early March, it may be worth calculating the profits of the business up to the end of February to avoid a last minute rush in the final days of the tax year. March's figures can then be calculated before the tax year ends.

This may be fairly easy to do if your business is VAT registered and the VAT returns give you a fairly good idea of the business's profit.

Chapter 31

Pension Planning for Landlords

When I started out writing this guide, I planned to conduct a comprehensive study comparing pensions and buy-to-let property. However, I quickly abandoned this idea for two reasons.

Firstly, a pension is not an asset, it's simply a 'wrapper' that protects the underlying assets from tax. Those assets are normally company shares and bonds and sometimes commercial property (but not residential property which is prohibited).

So any comparison between pensions and buy-to-let ultimately boils down to a comparison between stock market investing and residential property investing.

Plenty of academics have conducted studies to see which asset class performs best but the results are sensitive to the time period under consideration and whether you include rents and dividends in the analysis.

The second reason why I decided not to spend time comparing pensions and buy-to-let property is that many property investors would simply not countenance investing in anything else. "Nothing beats bricks and mortar," goes the popular mantra.

I've lost count of the number of times I've heard the phrase "my properties are my pension".

Having said this, some landlords may wish to make pension contributions to *complement* their property investments.

For example, if your properties are generating a lot of rental income you may have a lot of spare cash sitting in a taxed account, especially if you are already making full use of your £20,000 annual ISA allowance.

If you don't need that surplus cash for your property business, putting some of it in a pension will allow it to grow tax free and further diversify your investments beyond property.

Pension contributions may also be worth making if your taxable property income pushes you into a higher tax bracket.

Remember mortgage interest is no longer a tax deductible expense, so many landlords will have taxable property income that is significantly higher than their true rental profits.

For example, if your taxable property income pushes your total income over the £100,000 threshold, you will start losing your personal allowance and once your income reaches £125,140 it will be taken away completely.

But making pension contributions reduces your 'adjusted net income' which claws back some of your personal allowance. As a result, making pension contributions while your income is in the £100,000-£125,140 tax bracket will generally provide you with 60% tax relief (see Chapter 21).

Similarly, if you are the highest earner in a household claiming child benefit you face paying the child benefit charge when your taxable income exceeds £60,000. The full charge is payable when your income reaches £80,000 (see Chapter 20).

Some landlords may find that it is their taxable property income that pushes them into the £60,000-£80,000 tax bracket and any pension contributions they make will reduce their adjusted net income, which will also reduce the child benefit charge.

As a result, they may be able to enjoy tax relief of between 47% (one child) and 66% (five children) on any pension contributions they make.

One thing pension contributions won't do, however, is remove assets from your estate for inheritance tax purposes because pensions will become subject to inheritance tax from 6th April 2027.

Landlords without Earnings

Everyone under 75 can make a gross pension contribution of up to £3,600 per year.

If you want to contribute more than this and receive tax relief your gross contributions must not exceed your 'earnings'. (There are also other restrictions on how much you can contribute, discussed elsewhere in this guide.)

Salaries and trading profits are earnings for this purpose, rental profits are not. If a landlord wants to make a pension contribution of more than £3,600 he must have sufficient earnings from other sources.

So this chapter is mainly relevant to landlords who also have salary income from another job or profits from another business.

Any pension contributions you are already making out of your salary or profits from another business will also have to be taken into account when deciding the overall level of your pension contributions.

Property Company Owners

Companies can get tax relief for pension contributions made on behalf of directors, regardless of the type of business carried on by the company.

Thus property company owners can often enjoy considerably larger pension contributions than full-time landlords who do not have 'earnings' from employment or self-employment.

Provided the company pension contribution, together with any other remuneration (e.g. salary) paid to the director is justified by the work they do for the company, it will be a tax-deductible expense, providing corporation tax relief at up to 26.5%.

This is one of the major benefits of holding rental properties in a company, although there are lots of other issues to consider when deciding whether to incorporate – see the Taxcafe guide *Using a Property Company to Save Tax* for further information.

Higher-Rate Tax Relief for Landlords

From 6th April 2027 onwards, property income is to be separated from other forms of income and subject to higher income tax rates.

Basic-rate taxpayers will pay 22%, higher-rate taxpayers will pay 42% and additional-rate taxpayers will pay 47%.

At the same time the tax reduction for residential interest and finance costs will be increased from 20% to 22%.

Higher-rate taxpayers who face paying 42% income tax on their property income may wonder whether they can also enjoy 42% tax relief on any pension contributions they make. Sadly, the answer is no: total tax relief will remain at 40%.

Such individuals will still enjoy basic-rate tax relief at just 20% (this is the amount added to your pension by the taxman).

Higher-rate tax relief is then calculated by giving the individual an increased basic-rate band. For someone whose income is made up of salary and rental income, this means some of their property income could end up being taxed at 22% instead of 42% (additional 20% tax relief), or some of their salary could end up taxed at 40% instead of 20% (also an additional 20% tax relief).

Whether it's the salary or the rental income that benefits from the increased basic-rate band depends on how much salary the individual has... but, either way, the additional relief enjoyed on pension contributions by higher rate taxpayers will remain the same: 20%.

Taken together with their basic rate tax relief, this means the total tax relief will be 40%.

Similar principles apply to ensure additional-rate taxpayers with property income will continue to enjoy a total of 45% tax relief, and not 47%.

Paying 40% Tax When You Retire

Pensions are generally most attractive when you enjoy income tax relief of 40% (or more) on your contributions but pay tax at 20% on your withdrawals.

Many landlords who hold onto their property investments when they retire will pay 40% or more income tax on their pension withdrawals, if they also have a significant amount of taxable property income.

This makes it less attractive for them to make pension contributions.

However, this does not necessarily mean pension contributions are not worth making. The money in the pension will grow tax free and up to 25% can be taken as a tax-free lump sum. Taken together, this still makes a pension investment more attractive than an ISA from a tax saving standpoint, especially if you are already making full use of your £20,000 ISA allowance anyway.

Paying Less Capital Gains Tax

Pension contributions can help you save capital gains tax when you sell assets like property.

How?

Capital gains are generally taxed at 24% if you are a higher-rate taxpayer but just 18% to the extent you are a basic-rate taxpayer.

When you make pension contributions the taxman gives you a bigger basic-rate band. This means more of your capital gains will be taxed at 18% instead of 24%, saving you 6%.

Coupled with the normal 20% basic-rate tax relief on pension contributions (the taxman's top up) this means individuals who make contributions to save capital gains tax can enjoy 26% tax relief.

Clearly that's not as attractive as the 40% tax relief that can be enjoyed when you make pension contributions to save *income tax*, but could be worthwhile in some circumstances.

Example

Billy has earnings of exactly £50,270 (the higher-rate threshold) and a taxable capital gain of £10,000. As things stand he will pay 24% capital gains tax on his gain (£2,400).

Let's say he invests £8,000 in his pension. The taxman will top this up with £2,000 of basic-rate tax relief, resulting in a gross pension contribution of £10,000.

With a £10,000 gross pension contribution his basic-rate band will be extended by £10,000 which means he will now pay 18% capital gains tax on his gain (£1,800).

In summary, Billy saves £600 capital gains tax. Coupled with £2,000 of basic-rate tax relief, he enjoys a total of 26% tax relief on his £10,000 pension contribution.

It's important to make some additional points about using pension contributions to save capital gains tax:

- If Billy ends up paying 40% income tax when he eventually withdraws the money from his pension this will wipe out the capital gains tax saving. But if he pays just 20% income tax when he withdraws the money he will end up better off overall.

- Billy is a basic-rate taxpayer. If you are a higher-rate taxpayer any pension contribution you make will possibly save you income tax but not any capital gains tax. For example, if Billy has earnings of £70,000 and a £10,000 capital gain, a £10,000 pension contribution will provide him with 40% income tax relief but he will pay 24% capital gains tax on his gain, just like any other higher-rate taxpayer. As it happens, this is a better outcome.

- Billy may be better off paying 24% capital gains tax and postponing his pension contribution if he thinks he will become a higher-rate taxpayer in the near future. This way he will enjoy 40% income tax relief instead of 26% income tax and capital gains tax relief.

- Making pension contributions to save capital gains tax is not necessary if you already have enough basic-rate band remaining to cover the gain. For example, if Billy has earnings of just £40,000, he will have £10,270 of spare basic-rate band (£50,270 - £40,000). He will pay 18% capital gains tax anyway and will not have to make a pension contribution to lower his CGT bill.

- If you make a pension contribution to reduce your capital gains tax bill, it's important to make sure you keep enough cash aside to settle your CGT liability.

- To make pension contributions you need to have "earnings" (typically salary income or profits from self employment). Many full-time landlords do not have any earnings and will be restricted to making a gross pension contribution of just £3,600 per year.

Finally, note that pension contributions can be used to reduce the CGT payable on other assets, not just residential property.

For further information about CGT on residential property, including the requirement to make a payment on account within 60 days, see the Taxcafe guide *How to Save Property Tax.*

Chapter 32

Putting Property into a Pension

Some business owners use a specialist SIPP or other pension plan to hold their business premises and in this chapter we'll take a look at some of the benefits and drawbacks.

Note that you can put *commercial property* into a pension but not residential property.

Companies that market property SIPPs often point to the following benefits:

- **Tax-free rent**. There is no income tax payable on the rent your business pays into your pension. These rent payments will also be a tax deductible expense for the business. The money will then continue to grow tax free inside your pension.

- **No capital gains tax**. When a property held inside a pension is sold there is no capital gains tax payable.

Although the ability to roll up rental income tax free inside a pension is very attractive, you must also never lose sight of the fact that all the money you eventually withdraw from your pension, over and above your tax-free lump sum, will be subject to income tax.

If you are a higher or additional-rate taxpayer at present, but expect to be a basic-rate taxpayer when you retire, it's possible you will pay no more than 20% income tax on your pension withdrawals. However, I suspect many of those who set up property SIPPs are wealthier individuals, who will pay at least 40% income tax on some of their pension withdrawals.

Similarly, although property held in a pension can be sold without incurring capital gains tax, when you eventually withdraw the capital gain most of it (at least 75%) will be subject to income tax, again possibly at 40% or more.

Alternatively, if you sell commercial property that you own *personally* you will be subject to capital gains tax at 24% if you are a higher-rate taxpayer.

In some cases a sale of business premises that you own personally will qualify for Business Asset Disposal Relief. If so, a tax rate of 18% applies from 6th April 2026. But the relief is restricted if your company has paid you rent at any time since 6th April 2008.

When comparing pension ownership with personal ownership it's also important to remember that you cannot withdraw any money from your pension until you are at least 55 (rising to 57 in 2028).

Inheritance Tax

From 6th April 2027 pensions will become subject to inheritance tax. This will make holding business premises (and other commercial property) inside a pension far less attractive than at present.

In fact, it's possible owning business premises inside a pension could lead to a higher inheritance tax bill than owning them personally.

This is because the draft legislation makes no provision for assets held inside a pension to qualify for business property relief. Thus it appears that such assets will be fully exposed to inheritance tax from 6th April 2027. By contrast, business premises held *outside* a pension will generally still qualify for at least some business property relief.

Having said this, many retirees will not qualify for business property relief if a commercial property they own personally is no longer used in their own business, for example if the business has been sold or wound up and the property is simply held as a retirement investment, rented out to someone else.

Similarly, if your own business ceases to occupy a property that is held in your pension, the property can be rented out to someone else and the rental income will continue to roll up tax free.

In both cases (personal and pension ownership) commercial property held as an investment would be fully exposed to inheritance tax.

There are also concerns surrounding payment of inheritance tax when property is held in a pension. If your pension holds a highly illiquid asset such as a commercial property, a significant challenge could be faced raising the necessary cash to settle any inheritance tax bill. Unlike land and buildings held directly by an individual, it currently seems that it will not be possible to pay the tax relating to property held in a pension in ten yearly instalments.

It may be possible to take steps to mitigate this problem, however. If the property is no longer being used by your business and is simply held as an investment, the property could be sold earlier, rather than held until death, with the proceeds invested in other more liquid investments.

Alternatively, if the property does not exceed, say, 60% of the total value of the pension fund, it should be possible to sell the other assets in the pension to foot the inheritance tax bill.

It must be stressed that the relevant legislation has not yet been finalised and it is, of course, more than a year until these changes are due to take place, so we may see some relaxation on these issues from the Government before then.

For further information about pensions and inheritance tax, see the Taxcafe guide *How to Save Inheritance Tax*.

Funding the Property Purchase

The purchase of a business property by a pension can be funded in several ways. Typically you will use your existing pension savings, topped up with fresh contributions (including company pension contributions if you run a company).

It is also possible for your pension fund to borrow money but only up to 50% of its net assets. For example, if you have pension savings of £100,000 an additional £50,000 can be borrowed.

Some pension providers allow a part share in a property to be acquired by the pension plan, with the balance owned outside the pension.

Several individuals can also pool their pension savings to collectively buy a property.

Selling Existing Property to a SIPP

If you already own the property you may be able to sell it to your SIPP (on commercial arms-length terms) and release a sizeable amount of cash from your pension savings.

Selling an existing property you own to your pension is likely to result in capital gains tax becoming payable (typically at 24%) if the property has risen in value since you bought it. It is unlikely Business Asset Disposal Relief would be available in such cases.

A sizeable capital gains tax bill may put off many existing property owners going down the pension route but others may still be tempted by the prospect of receiving a large cash payment out of their pension savings.

The transfer may also result in a stamp duty land tax bill and VAT may also be payable in certain circumstances, although it may be possible to claim a VAT refund.

In Specie Contributions

Properties have in the past been transferred into pensions as *in specie* pension contributions, with the member claiming income tax relief. In specie contributions are no longer permitted following a clamp down by HMRC because of perceived abuse.

Costs and other Formalities

Not all pension providers deal with property purchases so you may need to transfer your existing pension savings to a specialist provider.

When your property is held inside a pension your business will have to be treated just like any other tenant, with no special favours, which means rent will have to be paid at a full market rate.

If rent is not paid this will be treated as an unauthorised payment by your pension and HMRC may levy a charge of 40% on you personally and a charge of up to 40% on the pension itself.

Property SIPPs are also much more expensive to run than those that only allow you to invest in traditional 'stocks and shares'.

Initial set up costs include legal fees, surveyor fees, lenders fees and fees to the pension company managing your SIPP.

Fees will have to be paid for regular rent revaluations and a third party property manager may have to be appointed to collect the rent from you.

These significant additional costs will eat into any tax savings you hope to achieve.

In summary, although there are benefits to holding business property inside a pension there are also significant drawbacks. Each case would have to be decided on its merits with help from a professional.

Part 8

Family Pension Planning

Chapter 33

Couples: Who Should Make the Pension Contributions?

Should you transfer money to your spouse or partner so that they can make pension contributions?

Even people who don't have any earnings (i.e. who don't work) can still make a small pension contribution and receive tax relief.

The limit is £3,600 per year with £2,880 coming from the individual and £720 from the taxman in basic-rate tax relief.

Is this worth doing? Some people think it is because, although there will only be basic-rate tax relief, the income that is ultimately withdrawn from the pension may be tax free if it is covered by the individual's income tax personal allowance, currently £12,570.

If your spouse or partner eventually receives a state pension, that income will probably use up some and perhaps all of their personal allowance. However, income can be withdrawn from private pensions up to 10 years' earlier.

Case Study

Rory is a higher-rate taxpayer and his wife Claire has a much lower income or doesn't work at all (whichever you prefer).

The couple want to make small additional pension contributions (for Claire these cannot exceed £3,600 per year gross if she doesn't work) and are trying to decide *who* should make them.

Rory will enjoy higher-rate tax relief if he makes the contributions BUT he expects to ultimately pay income tax at 20% when he withdraws the money. Claire will only enjoy basic-rate tax relief if she makes the contribution BUT she hopes to pay 0% tax when she withdraws the money (thanks to her income tax personal allowance).

Let's assume the couple want to save an additional £1,000 this year. If Claire makes the contribution the taxman will add £250 of basic-rate tax relief, producing a gross pension contribution of £1,250.

Rory can make a net cash contribution of £1,333. The taxman will add £333 of basic-rate relief, resulting in a gross contribution of £1,666. Rory will also receive £333 of higher-rate tax relief (£1,666 x 20%), so the net cost to him is also £1,000 (£1,333 cash contribution - £333 higher-rate relief).

Rory has an extra £1,666 going into his pension, whereas Claire only has £1,250. Rory's pension contribution is 33% bigger than Claire's.

Withdrawing Income

How much money will Claire or Rory have when they ultimately withdraw this money from their pensions and pay any income tax due?

We can ignore any investment growth as it doesn't affect the overall outcome. We will also ignore any future contributions to keep the example simple. We will also assume they can both take 25% tax-free, with the remaining 75% subject to income tax when withdrawn.

Their positions are summarised in Table 8. The total after tax includes the tax-free lump sum and the income remaining after paying income tax at either 0%, 20% or 40%.

The example is simplistic but does offer some interesting insights:

When Rory Should Make the Contributions

If Rory pays 20% income tax when he withdraws the additional contribution (remember he has other pension savings so this isn't guaranteed) he will end up with £1,416. If Claire pays 0% income tax (thanks to her personal allowance) she will end up with £1,250. Rory ends up with 13% more money.

So the first conclusion is: Rory should probably make the additional contributions, even if Claire will pay no tax.

It may be even more important that Rory makes the additional contributions if Claire has existing pension savings that are likely to use up her personal allowance or if she will eventually receive taxable income from other sources. If Claire ends up paying 20% tax she could end up with £1,062 compared with Rory's £1,416. Rory ends up with 33% more money in this scenario.

Table 8
Couples Pension Planning
Who Should Make Contributions?

	Higher-rate relief on contributions	Basic-rate relief on contributions
	£	£
"Pension pot"	1,666	1,250
25% Tax-free	416	312
75% Taxable	1,250	938
Total after tax:		
After-tax @ 0%	1,666	1,250
After-tax @ 20%	1,416	1,062
After-tax @ 40%	1,166	875

When Claire Should Make the Contributions

What if Rory, like Claire, will not receive higher-rate tax relief on any additional pension contributions, only basic-rate tax relief? This could happen if his existing pension contributions are already equal to the amount of income he has taxed at 40% (see Chapter 4 for an explanation).

In this case Rory could end up with £1,062 compared with Claire's potentially tax-free £1,250. Claire ends up with 18% more money in this scenario.

So the second conclusion is this: Claire should perhaps make the additional contributions if Rory cannot obtain any more higher-rate tax relief.

But if Rory does enjoy higher-rate tax relief on any additional contributions, Claire will only end up better off than him if she pays 0% tax **and** he pays 40% tax (for example, if he has already built up significant pension savings).

In reality, Claire may only be able to pay 0% tax in a very limited number of circumstances, for example if her existing pension savings are quite modest and any additional pension contributions she now makes are withdrawn before she reaches state pension age.

(Note, even if Claire is not currently working she will be building up state pension entitlement if she has children under 12 and qualifies for child benefit.)

In the worst case scenario Claire will pay 40% tax when she withdraws the additional pension contributions. This could happen if, for example, she receives a significant inheritance later on and those assets generate a lot of taxable income.

Higher Rates of Tax Relief

If Claire receives child benefit and Rory's adjusted net income is still in the £60,000-£80,000 bracket, he should probably be the one making the additional pension contributions (see Chapter 20). This will allow him to reduce the child benefit tax charge and enjoy 47% or more tax relief on his pension contributions.

If Rory's adjusted net income is still in the £100,000-£125,140 bracket he should probably be the one making the additional pension contributions because he will be able to enjoy up to 60% tax relief (see Chapter 21).

Family Tax Planning and Other Issues

It's worth pointing out that Claire may have *non-tax* reasons for wanting to make pension contributions, for example if she feels this gives her greater financial security.

It's worth noting that there are other things the couple can do to make use of Claire's tax-free personal allowance if she is not currently working. For example, rental properties, savings accounts and other assets could be placed in her name, as could any money the couple may eventually inherit.

Lifetime ISAs

These are discussed in detail in Part 3. Those under 40 can save up to £4,000 per year in a Lifetime ISA with a £1,000 Government bonus.

If Claire is under 40 she may prefer to put her money into a Lifetime ISA instead of a pension because the upfront tax relief is currently the same as a pension BUT all her withdrawals will be completely tax free.

Similarly, if Rory expects to be a higher-rate taxpayer when he retires he may be better off investing his additional savings in a Lifetime ISA.

Note the future of the Lifetime ISA is currently in doubt. The Government has announced that it will be abolished but existing account holders are expected to be allowed to continue contributing.

Chapter 34

Pensions for Children and Grandchildren

"When I was a boy of 14, my father was so ignorant I could hardly stand to have the old man around. But when I got to be 21, I was astonished at how much the old man had learned in seven years."
Mark Twain

Everyone under the age of 75 can make a pension contribution of £3,600 per year and receive basic-rate tax relief (which currently reduces the net cost to £2,880).

This means minor children can benefit from pension contributions made by their parents or grandparents.

Many pension providers have special pension plans for minors, like the Junior SIPP from Hargreaves Lansdown. According to HMRC, around 60,000 children under 18 years of age are benefiting from this tax break.

Making pension contributions on behalf of a minor child could be a wonderful way to leave an asset of lasting value that cannot be frittered away, at least not until the child is a responsible adult!

These contributions have the added bonus of being possibly exempt from inheritance tax, being covered by either the £3,000 annual exemption or the regular gifts out of income exemption.

A pension contribution made on behalf of a minor child could grow into a significant nest egg. For example, let's say you make 18 annual contributions of £2,880 starting in the year a child is born. Each contribution will be topped up with £720 of basic-rate tax relief (even though the child doesn't pay any income tax), producing a gross pension contribution of £3,600 per year.

If we assume that the investments in the pension grow by 7% per year, just before the child's 18th birthday, when the last contribution is made, the pension pot will be worth £122,397. However, that's not the end of the story. The money will continue to compound tax free until the child reaches the minimum retirement age. For example, when the child is 58 the pension pot could be worth close to £2 million.

Of course, these figures aren't adjusted for inflation. If some inflation adjustments are made they could still end up with a pension pot worth several hundred thousand pounds in today's money, which is still a tidy sum.

We don't know what the minimum retirement age will be many decades from now – it could be a lot higher than 58 – and that is perhaps one major drawback of contributing to a pension so early.

Junior ISAs

Just like normal ISAs, money grows tax free but there is no upfront tax relief, as there is with pension contributions.

The annual limit is £9,000, a lot higher than a junior SIPP.

Unlike regular ISAs, money cannot be withdrawn until the child reaches age 18. From that date the junior ISA becomes an adult ISA and the child can do what he or she likes with the money.

Junior SIPP vs Junior ISA

Most children or grandchildren would probably prefer you to contribute to a junior ISA that they can access from age 18. After all, they will face numerous financial challenges between the age of 18 and retirement age: university fees, cars, mortgages, childcare costs etc.

They could also take their junior ISA savings and gradually invest them in an "adult" SIPP when they are working, with full higher-rate tax relief (junior SIPPs only enjoy basic-rate tax relief).

However, there is a risk money saved in a junior ISA will be frittered away if it can be accessed at the tender age of 18. Putting money in a locked box has its benefits and they may thank you for it one day!

www.ingramcontent.com/pod-product-compliance
Lightning Source LLC
LaVergne TN
LVHW022201200926
848481LV00006B/1811